Business Accounting System Implementation

Asok K Nadhani

www.bpbonline.com

First Edition 2025

ISBN: 978-93-6589-615-2

LIMITS OF LIABILITY AND DISCLAIMER OF WARRANTY

Author's Note

This publication is designed for business organisations that are either implementing an accounting system for the first time, or seeking to enhance and expand their existing systems by integrating additional functional areas and leveraging new advancements.

Through 30+ years of experience as a professional accountant and Business Software consultant, I have also authored 25+ books on accounting software and related subjects. In this book, I share valuable insights drawn from my experiences and the challenges encountered by organizations in selection and implementation of accounting systems.

However, I believe that users are uniquely positioned to articulate the practical aspects of business systems. Therefore, I invite professionals involved in managing accounting and finance operations across various organizations, to share their experiences, suggestions, and advice by contacting me at dvidyamail@gmail.com. Together, we can exchange ideas, enhance knowledge and explore exciting professional work opportunities, for our mutual benefit.

I have also established a collaborative education website, dvidya.com, dedicated to students, educators, authors, Accounting Professionals, fostering learning and providing opportunities for income generation through work-from-home services. I invite you to visit the site and feel free to reach out with your queries and valuable feedback.

My clients often need digital creators for their social media sites. Interested persons may email, giving details of their work experience, skillsets, and profile links.

— Asok K Nadhani

Preface

Accounting Software Myth

Software marketing professionals often perpetuate the misconception, that merely installing software will effortlessly resolve all accounting tasks and challenges. However, the implementation of a computerized system is a complex endeavor. If not meticulously planned, it can lead to more issues than it seeks to address.

Introduction of Accounting Software System

Some organizations may introduce a computerized accounting system for the first time, while others may transition to a new system.

This book guides to evaluate the objectives, evolve appropriate solution, plan for collection and proper structuring of initial data, and effectively implement an accounting system within an enterprise, to achieve desired outcomes.

Enterprise Accounting Software System

An Enterprise Accounting System encompasses a wide range of accounting functions across the three M resources: Money (financial accounting), Materials (inventory accounting), and Manpower (payroll accounting), all synchronized with tax accounting (GST, TDS, TCS). A comprehensive Enterprise Accounting System designed for organizations of varying sizes, industries, and legal forms, must offer easy customization (or configuration) to meet organisation's specific needs.

This book elucidates the structure of each functional module, the interrelationships of data between modules, and the overall integration of component systems, in a standalone computer as well as across multiple computing units connected via LAN or the internet.

Selection of Right Business Accounting Software

This Book provides a comprehensive overview of various genres of major Indian Accounting Software, targeted for each Business Enterprise forms and sizes, like, Enterprise Accounting Systems tailored for large and medium-sized organizations; Integrated Accounting Systems designed for medium and small enterprises; Invoicing and General Ledger Accounting Systems suitable for small businesses; and GST Invoicing Systems aimed at merchant retailers, highlighting the key features.

It also discusses model features of Business Accounting Software, and brief overview of about 20+ major Accounting Software available in the market, to make the right buying decision for software acquisition and plan for implementation.

AI Accounting Software

Finally, a section is devoted to AI (Artificial Intelligence), tools and AI-assisted accounting systems, its latest development, trends and application in business accounts automation and management, followed by brief outline of few selected AI Accounting Software tools, making the book most contemporary and technologically updated.

— Asok K Nadhani

Table of Contents

CHAPTER 1
Introduction to Business Accounting

What is Business Accounting

Business accounting is the process of recording, summarizing, and analyzing a company's financial transactions to show financial performance and health, by tracking income, expenses, assets, and liabilities.

Purpose of Business Accounting

Business Accounting is necessary to comply with legal requirements, prepare financial statements, and make informed decisions. It is also required to give fair and correct financial reports to stakeholders like investors, regulators, and creditors. It helps to secure funding from investors and financial institutions to efficiently run and grow the business

Business Accounting System

- **Manual Accounting System:** Business Accounting started with writing transactions in manually written Books of Accounts. The transactions are recorded in Journal Books, which form the basic transactions data. Ledger Books and all Accounting statements are compiled by posting, collation, balancing accounting figures from the transactions date from the Journal. So, all accounting tasks and reporting are repeatedly done from by writing the same transaction data in various formats. It is a mundane task, time consuming, human error prone.

- **Computerised Accounting System:** Unlike Manual system of writing Accounting data and maintaining Books of Accounts and preparing Accounting reports, Computerized accounting systems offer tools for recording, organizing, and reporting financial data electronically.

  The Transactions data are input for once. All Accounting Books and Reports are generated instantly and correctly, by the Accounting Software.

Business Accounting Software

- **Evolution of Business Accounting Software:** Business accounting software has progressed significantly from its origins as a simple bookkeeping tool, to advanced systems capable of performing financial reporting, budgeting, and tax preparation. With the advent of cloud-based systems and ERP (Enterprise Resource Planning) tools, accounting information are accessible from anywhere, offering real-time insights, collaboration features, and improved data security.
- **Importance of Business Accounting Software:** Business accounting software is essential for modern business management, integrating diverse operations like accounting, finance, inventory, payroll, and compliance. It provides a unified platform for streamlined processes and data-driven decision-making, ensuring regulatory compliance while reducing manual errors.
- **Strategic Impact on Business Growth:** An integrated accounting solution empowers businesses to adapt to market changes, strategize effectively, and achieve sustained growth. It supports competitive advantage by streamlining operations and facilitating better access to critical financial data, ensuring businesses remain agile and prepared for challenges.
- **Key Benefits of Accounting Software:**
  - o **Efficiency and Transparency:** Enhances transparency, minimizes redundancy, and improves operational efficiency.

- o **Real-Time Insights:** Offers businesses actionable insights for informed decision-making and strategic planning.
- o **Scalability:** Adapts to organizational growth without requiring a complete system overhaul.
- o **Regulatory Compliance:** Ensures adherence to legal requirements and standards.
- o **Collaboration:** Promotes cross-departmental collaboration by aligning teams with company goals.

Business Accounting Software Types

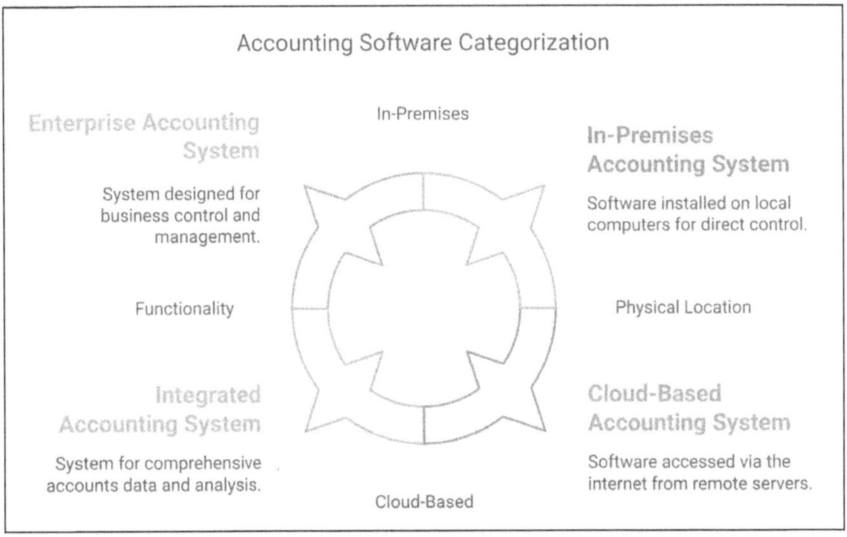

Based on Functionality and Integration, Accounting Software may be broadly classified into following types

- **Enterprise Accounting System (EAS):** Enterprise Accounting Systems are typically designed for large organizations, governments, or businesses with distributed operations. These systems are technologically complex and integrate all organizational resources to provide a unified and holistic view.
  - o **Advanced Integration:** Supports external systems like Client Portals, CRM, HRM, Project Management tools, Payment Processing, Messaging Systems, Alerts, and Dashboards.
  - o **Comprehensive Functionality:** Offers graphical insights, infographics, and control features to support data-driven decision-making.

- **Focus on Business Control:** Utilizes accounting data for real-time business management, decision-making, and operational control.
- **Robust Scalability:** Handles large transaction volumes and supports complex organizational structures, ensuring compliance with industry regulations.
- **ERP Integration:** Often integrates with Enterprise Resource Planning systems, to streamline operations across departments and locations.

EAS emphasizes proactive control and future-oriented decision-making by leveraging historical data to predict and manage intended outcomes.

- **Integrated Accounting System (IAS):** Integrated Accounting Systems are tailored for small to medium-sized organizations, providing affordable and cohesive solution covering multiple functional areas.
  - **Modular Structure:** Divides business resources into modules such as:
    - **Money:** Financial Accounting
    - **Materials:** Inventory Management
    - **Manpower:** Payroll Accounting
    - **Taxation:** Compliance and Reporting
  - **Seamless Integration:** Modules work cohesively to present a complete picture of business operations.
  - **Real-Time Updates:** Information from various supporting modules and functional areas automatically flow into the system, ensuring up-to-date information.
  - **Holistic View:** Provides a consolidated perspective of operations, enabling informed decision-making.
  - **Affordable Solution:** Suitable for organizations seeking enhanced collaboration and functionality using simpler tools.

IAS primarily focuses on recording and analyzing historical data to assess the business's past performance and inform current decisions.

EAS & IAS- Key Distinction

- **Enterprise Accounting System (EAS):** Centers on *control and proactive management*, using data to guide future actions.
- **Integrated Accounting System (IAS):** Concentrates on *historical analysis*, providing insights into past and present operations for informed decision-making.

From the perspective of ownership and location of Data and Software, computerised accounting software may be broadly classified as:

- **In-Premises Accounting System:** The software is installed and runs directly on a business's own computers or servers within its office. All data is stored locally in company's computer system. So, the organisation has complete control over the system and data, But accessing the system remotely might be difficult. It is a traditional setup up preferred by businesses with stable office environment and specific security needs.
- **Cloud Accounting System:** The software is installed in remote cluster of servers (so the name Cloud), connected through Internet, accessible through a web browser, from any place, any compatible device, any time. It provides instant connectivity with the world at large, easily scalable and can embrace the latest technological development quickly and seamlessly.

  In Premises Accounting system – Key Points:

  - Installed on the business's own computers and servers.
  - All data are stored locally, giving the business full control over the system and its data.
  - Organisation must update the system and take Data Back Up regularly.
  - Management must install the security system

  Cloud-Based Accounting Systems – Key Points:

  - Hosted on remote servers and accessible online from any compatible device.
  - Data storage, Back Up and system updates are managed by the provider.
  - Higher security features.
  - Easy scalability and remote access but requires a stable internet connection

Embracing Cloud Accounting System

Though Cloud Accounting System are gradually proliferating due to various technological advancements and benefits, there are still apprehension in embracing Cloud System. Business organisations often look down on non visible virtual cloud space as something alien to trust, for keeping sacrosanct business data. We list the key apprehensions and fears about Cloud System.

- **Internet Connectivity:** Constant internet is needed for cloud accounting. Organisations fear that work would get stalled when there is no Internet connection. However, there is constant technological development. Reliable options like 5G, fiber, and future satellite tech ensure consistent access.
- **Data Security:** Cloud accounting raises data security concerns of data being accessed by hackers. Cloud Systems are safeguarded by high standards, even better than orgniastions own security system.
- **Lack of Awareness:** Small businesses often lack digital literacy, hindering cloud adoption. Largest nationwide system like Banks, telecom, Government Tax services, Railways. Education are successfully running on Cloud Systems.
- **Fear of Job:** Accountants often resist cloud transition, fearing job loss. All Technological advancements, which empower people and make their work and life easier and simpler, would ultimately be accepted by people. Employes must be encouraged to learn new things for career improvement. So, this apprehension is unfounded.
- **Vendor Lock-In:** The software and data is not owned by the organisation. The service providers may do arms twisting to pay more, or the organisation may stop their business altogether.
- **Pay-Per-User Model:** The total service cost is unpredictable as it varies with the usage. Over time, the usage would constantly grow. However, more usage, means better utilisation of service reaping more benefits.
- **Migration to Cloud System:** Business already using On-premises system often hesitate to move to cloud based system due to apprehensions cited above. They also fear interruption of their current on-going work.

However, transitioning to the cloud is often facilitated by the vendor through easy data migration process. Modern cloud platforms smoothly integrate functional areas like accounting, inventory, payroll, etc.

Indian Accounting Software- Key Features

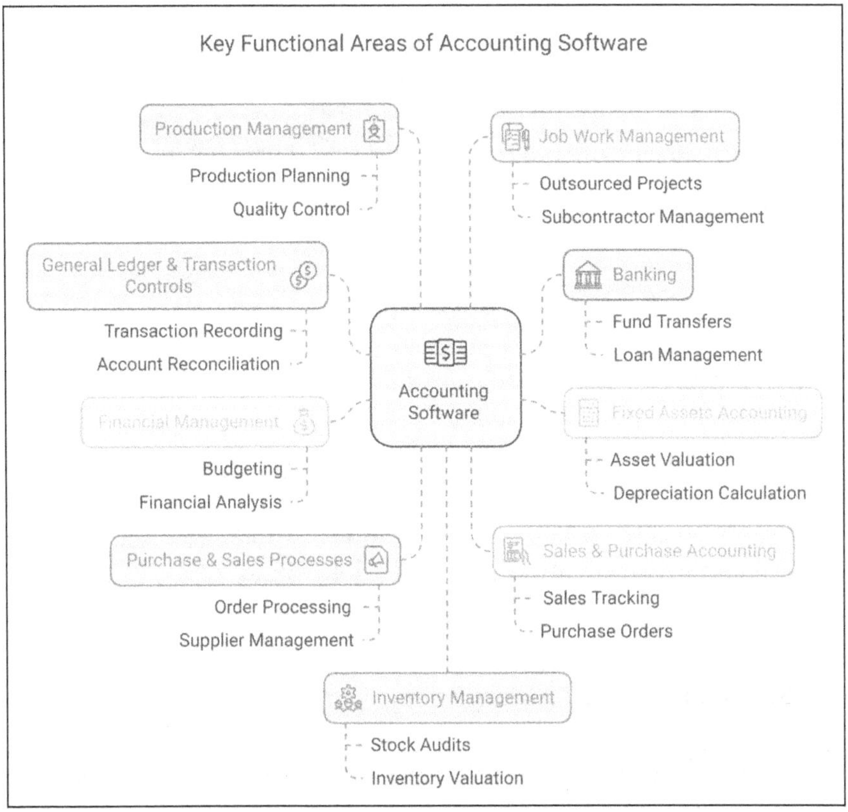

Below is a summary essential features developed and tailored for Indian Business Practice. This may be used as guidance for evaluation and selection of right product, suitable for the organisation. In the following chapters, we discuss in more details about these features.

General Ledger & Transaction Controls

- **Chart of Accounts:** Flexible and hierarchical with industry-specific templates.
- **Transaction Control Setup:** Custom voucher types, numbering schemes, and recurring transaction automation.

Banking

- **Bank Reconciliation:** Automated bank feed and easy reconciliation.
- **Cheque Printing:** Customised cheque printing and cancellation options.
- **Payment Gateway Integration:** Multiple gateway support for smooth money transfers.
- **Multi-Currency Accounts:** Automated currency exchange rate updates, concurrent currency reporting, Forex Gain / Loss Accounting.

Fixed Assets Accounting

- **Fixed Assets Records:** Classified Assets data with assets unique ID, complete Asset details, acquisition cost, Disposal / Scrapping of Assets, Capitalised Expenses.
- **Depreciation:** Depreciation Methods, rates, yearwise & cumulative Deprecation computaion, WDV.
- **Fixed Assets Reports:** Accounting report of Acquisitions, Disposals, Depreciation, Year end Book Values

Financial Management

- **Budgeting & Cash Management:** Track budgets, Cash flow, and cash movements.
- **Cost & Profit Centers:** Analyze financial performance across cost and profit centers.

Purchase & Sales Processes

- **Purchase Orders & Invoice:** Compare Vendor's Prices, Issue & Track Purchase orders, Delivery reminders, Materials Acknowledgement & Inspection, Materials Receipts, Purchase Invoice.
- **Sales Invoicing:** Customise Sales Order & Invoice contents & layout, Sales Orders & Invoice,
- **Point-of-Sale (POS) System:** Fast billing, multiple discounts, special sales, Reward Coupons, multiple payment modes.

Sales & Purchase Accounting

- **Accounts Receivable/Payable:** Track outstanding bills, automated reminders, and communication history.
- **Supplier & Vendor Management:** Comprehensive tracking of purchase orders, invoices, and vendor bills.
- **Customer Relationship Management:** Manage interactions, orders, and follow-ups with customers and suppliers.

Production Management

- **Bill of Materials:** Define standard input/output, track Consumption & production variances.
- **Production Stages:** Set up production stages, cycle of Input Materials & Output Products, Finished Products Packing.

Job Work

- **Job Work In:** Job Contracts, Receipt of Materials from Principals, Consumption of Materials, Return of Materials, Job Production, Delivery to Principals, Job Charges Receivables, Jobbing Reports,
- **Job Work Out:** Job Contracts, Issue of Materials to Jobbers, Return of Materials from Jobbers, Job Production Receipts, Job Charges Payables, Jobbing Reports.

Inventory Management

- **Warehouse:** Multi level Multi Storage locations organisations. Materials movements & Stock
- **Barcoding:** Create Bar Code system, Print barcodes or QR codes with item descriptions and expiry dates.
- **Inventory Controls:** Stock level management, reorder alerts, and batch tracking, Physical Stock Verification, Reconciliation, Adjustments, Wastage & Obsolescence

Tax Accounting & Compliance

- **GST Accounting:** GST set up, GST Invoicing, e-Invoice, e-way bills, GSTR Reconciliation, GSTR Uploads, GST Payments, GSTR filings.
- **TCS Accounting:** TCS Invoicing, Tax deposit, Statutory Returns Filing

- **TDS Accounting:** Automated TDS calculation, deduction, Tax deposit, TDS Certificates, Statutory Returns Filing.

Payroll Management

- **Payroll Accounting:** Payroll Integration, Employee Data, Employee Attendance / Production, Payroll Processing, Pay Slips, Pay Reports.
- **Payroll Statutory Reports:** Payroll Statutory Reports (EPF, ESI, FPS, P Tax, I Tax etc.), deposit to Government,

Additional Features

- **E-commerce Integration:** E-commerce invoicing and payment gateway setups.
- **Project Management:** Track time, tasks, and bill clients directly.
- **Data Migration:** Import data from other accounting software and streamline migration.

This features summary offers an overview of Indian business accounting software features, tailored to help managers efficiently manage day-to-day operations, finances, compliance, and reporting.

CHAPTER 2

Planning for Implementing Business Accounting Software

An accounting software system is a long-term investment, with significant commitments in time, money, and effort. Selecting a solution that aligns well with current and anticipated needs reduces the risk of costly replacements down the line, ensuring the software remains a valuable asset for the organization.

Implementing a computerised business accounting system requires careful pre-planning. The first step is assessing the company's needs and selecting software that aligns with its size, complexity, and compliance requirements.

A robust training plan must be developed to familiarise staff with the new system. The businesses should establish a clear timeline for implementation, including testing phases to ensure all aspects of the system function correctly and smoothly before moving fully to the new Computerised System.

For large companies with established technical expertise, an Enterprise Accounting System (EAS) may be viable choice, enabling sophisticated financial insight. Midsize organizations integrating multiple functions may benefit from an Integrated Accounting System (IAS), which can streamline operations across departments. Small businesses focusing on invoicing, accounts receivable, and core financial tasks may find an Invoicing & Accounting System most practical.

Below are key steps to guide the evaluation and selection of a suitable accounting system for any organization:

Evaluation and Selection of Right Business Accounting System

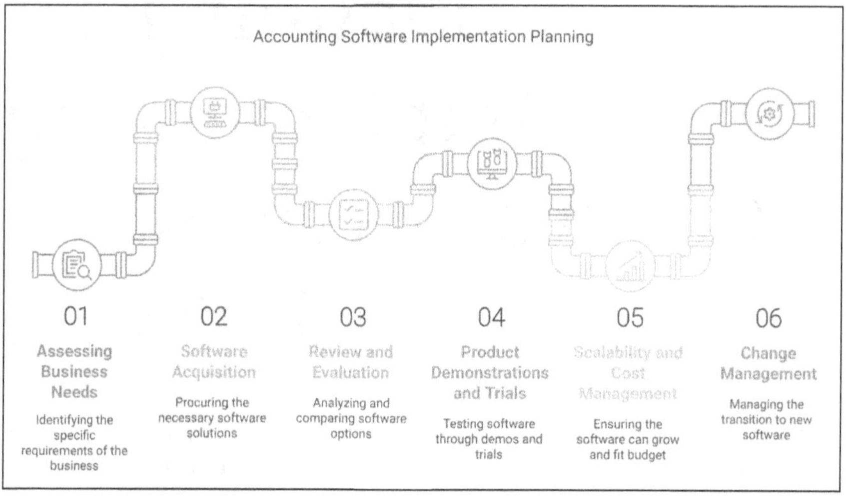

1. **Assessing Business Needs:** First and foremost, identify essential and desired features to support current and future business needs. Key persons across departments should be involved to evolve comprehensive alignment on system requirements.
2. **Software Acquisition:** From the point of view of software acquisition, Accounting software may be categorised in two classes. Proprietary Customised Systems and Ready made Packaged Standard System.
    - **Custom Software:** Tailored to an organisation's unique needs, custom software provides precise functionality but typically requires a significant investment in time and money.
    - **Standard Packaged Software:** Ready-made solutions offer affordability and immediate deployment, though they vary by industry, features, price, and technology. A detailed comparison of options is essential to find a system that aligns closely with business needs.

3. **Review and Evaluation:** While reviewing software, consider factors like features, initial and ongoing costs, scalability, ease of use, and future updates. Real-world performance insights from peer reviews and recommendations, provide valuable context on vendor support and software reliability.
4. **Product Demonstrations and Trials:** Just don't go on Marketing talks and brands. Take advantage of free trials and demos offered by vendors to evaluate functionality with realistic business scenarios. Use both sample and actual data to test the software's capabilities. This phase also allows opportunity for assessment of vendor's customer support, training, and implementation resources, in long-term perspective.
5. **Scalability and Cost Management:** Choose scalable software to meet future business growth. Apart from initial purchase cost, consider long-term costs like support, maintenance, user licenses, integrations, and upgrades. A robust software solution should accommodate evolving needs, providing sustained value over time.
6. **Change Management:** Transitioning to a new accounting system can be challenging, particularly with resistance from employees accustomed to existing system. Comprehensive training, awareness of resulting benefits for the organsiation growth and employee upskill would encourage smooth transition, especially for businesses without an internal IT team.

Business Accounting Software Implementation Challenges

Implementing an accounting system involves unique challenges. Accurate data migration is critical; errors in transferring data from legacy systems can often be intimidating. Organizations should allocate time and resources to ensure data accuracy, train employees, and manage the change process effectively.

Planning & Implementing Computerised Accounting System – Key Steps

Implementing a computerised accounting system requires a strategic, structured approach to ensure alignment with business goals and to maximize efficiency. Here are key steps for effective planning and implementation:

1. **Define Business Needs:** Identify the essential accounting functions—such as financial records, accounts receivable/payable, inventory control, payroll, and third-party accounts—that the system should support. Also, consider advanced needs like multi-currency support, multiple warehouses, customized reports, and manufacturing or asset tracking features.
2. **Set Clear Objectives:** Establish specific goals, like improving financial accuracy, reducing manual work, and accelerating invoicing, cash management, and reporting. These objectives will guide your implementation decisions.
3. **Assess Current Processes:** Review existing accounting workflows to determine how the new system can enhance accuracy, streamline tasks, and address current inefficiencies.
4. **Budget Planning:** Define a budget covering initial costs and ongoing expenses, including software licenses, hardware upgrades, and maintenance.
5. **Software Evaluation and Selection:** Compare available accounting software options based on features, cost, scalability, and ease of use. Select the one that best matches your operational needs.
6. **Vendor Support and Maintenance:** Choose a provider with dependable support, timely updates, and ongoing maintenance services to ensure system reliability.
7. **Statutory Compliance:** Ensure the system complies with relevant regulatory requirements, such as tax laws (e.g., GST, TDS, TCS) & statutory rules.
8. **System Integration:** Verify that the software integrates well with other applications (e.g. Excel sheets) allowing data flow across the system, and devices (like Bar Code / QR Code Readers, Cash Drawers, Thermal Printers etc).

9. **Customization:** Determine if the software can be customized for specific needs, such as unique reporting formats or industry-specific requirements. Evaluate if customization can be done in-house or through vendor only.
10. **Data Migration Planning:** Plan for secure and accurate transfer of existing digital data into the new system, ensuring that no critical information is lost.
11. **Implementation Timeline:** Develop a phased implementation timeline with key milestones for data migration, system testing, and employee training.
12. **User Training:** Conduct comprehensive training for all system users to ensure a smooth transition and minimize errors.
13. **Role-Based Access Control:** Implement role-based permissions to control user access, allowing each employee to access only the data relevant to their role.
14. **Testing and Trial Runs:** Conduct trial runs to test system functionality and identify any issues before full deployment.
15. **Data Backup and Restore:** Set up regular data backups and test data restoration processes to ensure data protection. Run mock drills to confirm that employees can handle backup and recovery procedures.
16. **Data Security:** Implement security features such as encryption and multi-factor authentication to protect sensitive financial data.
17. **Change Management:** Communicate the benefits of the new system to employees to reduce resistance. Offer support to facilitate the transition.
18. **Monitor and Evaluate:** Continuously monitor system performance post-implementation to ensure it meets objectives and addresses any emerging issues promptly.
19. **Scalability for Future Growth:** Confirm that the software can scale with your business, allowing additional users, increased transactions, and new functionalities as the business grows.
20. **Post-Implementation Review:** Conduct a thorough review after deployment to assess system performance and make any necessary adjustments to optimize results.

By following this structured approach, businesses can ensure a smooth transition to a computerised accounting system that aligns with operational needs, improves efficiency, and supports future growth.

CHAPTER 3

Business Accounting Software– General Features

Here we discuss about essential and common features of Accounting Software. These should be critically reviewed and used as guidance for evaluation and selection of right product, suitable for the organisation. In the following chapters, we discuss in more details about these features.

Modular Structure Accounting System

The software should be modular is design. The core module at the centre is essential part, while all other functional module may be optional and connect to the core module. The core module is the controlling part. All functional modules get connected to the Core Module. The details of the Core module are further explained in next chapter.

- **Core General Ledger Module:** The General Ledger (GL) forms the central core of the accounting system. All other functional modules are synced and linked to the GL for seamless integration.
- **Functional Modules:** Functional Modules like Inventory, Tax Accounts, Payroll, etc. Each module operates independently while maintaining connectivity to the core GL.
- **Seamless Integration:** Activity in functional module causes real time updates across the entire system.

- **Flexibility in Use:** Specific functional module may be adopted or activated based as required. The modular design enables customization and scalability as business needs evolve.
- **Adaptability and Expansion:** Flexible Modular design to accommodate future changes or expansions. Seamless change in one module without adversely affecting other modules. Expansion of system with business growth.

Flexible Software Pricing Scheme

Modular pricing allows businesses to pay for only the modules or services they need. Facilitates affordability for smaller businesses while ensuring scalability for larger operations.

- **On-Premises Software Pricing:** Involves a one-time consolidated payment at installation, regardless of usage volume. Price may vary based on the number of functionalities or modules included.
- **Cloud-Based Software Pricing:** Costs are based on usage volume and selected functionalities, as payment is for services rather than software. Offers scalability with costs increasing as usage or module requirements grow over time.
- **Software Licensing Fees:** On-premises software requires a one-time licensing fee, and also annual maintenance and support fee. Cloud based software involves regular subscription payments that include usage and maintenance costs.
- **Cost Estimation:** Users should estimate initial costs for low usage and plan for gradual cost increases as usage expands over time. Proper planning ensures affordability and aligns software costs with business growth.
- **Free Trial Plans:** On-site software often provides trial versions with either full features for a limited time (e.g., 15 or 30 days) or restricted functionality for an unlimited period. Cloud Based software may provide limited functionality, for a limited period, to test and evaluate the software. Free & Trial Plans enables users to evaluate the software with real-time data to assess its suitability.

Software Renewals & Discontinuance

- **Renewals:** Normally vendors appreciate auto renewals, (through Auto payment of renewal fees) so that the user enjoys continuous service, updates and support, without any interruption.
- **Discontinuance:** To discontinue the service, user must intimate with vendor in advance.
    - **On-site Software Discontinuance:** In case of on- site system, the software and data remains with the user. In such case, the vendor will stop software upgrades and support service. But user may continue to the software for unlimited period.
    - **Cloud based service Discontinuance:** In case of Cloud Based Service, the user may not be able to access the system anymore. At best, the user may copy the reports in their computer, but not the data, because the user is paying for the service only. So this should be kept in mind by opting for cloud-based system. On Discontinuance of on-line service, the user may ask the vendor to remove their data from the vendor's cloud system.

Help Manuals and Documents in Accounting Software

- **Comprehensive Help Resources:** High-quality on-line and off line manuals should be provided to cover all aspects of the system, including detailed explanations of features and processes, with examples and use cases of real life practical applications
- **Multiple Formats:** Manuals in multiple formats, like text-based documents, Blog posts, audio guides and video tutorials for versatile learning.
- **FAQ:** Manuals should include FAQs on popular and practical topics, for quick reference
- **Regular Updates:** Manuals and help documents should be continuously updated to reflect changes, new features, and improvements in the system.
- **Ease of Accessibility:** Documents should be easy to locate and navigate, ensuring even non-technical users can quickly find the needed guidance.

Software Support Service

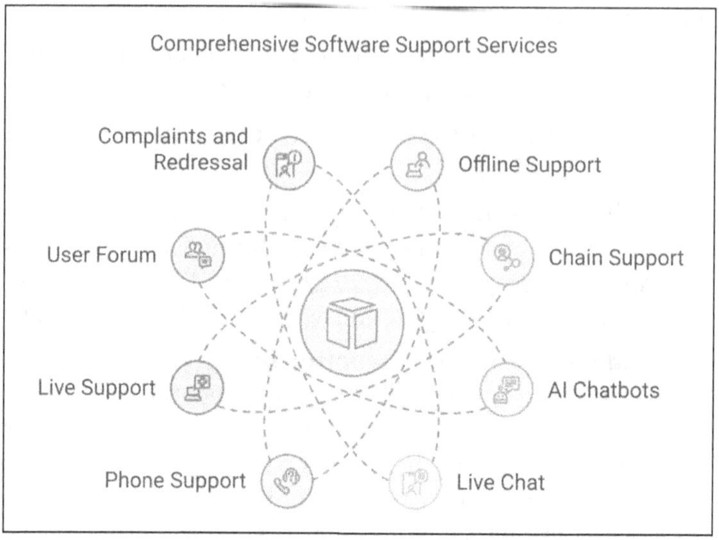

Software support is integral part of Software service. It is obligatory for the vendor to provide support service to registered paid users.

A software is useless without active vendor support. Users may review the suitability of a software before purchase, but quality and timely Support Services cannot be checked beforehand. It is a good practice to inquire about the support service quality from other uses of the software. Support services are provided in various forms. Some vendors may restrict the support service to FREE users, while some vendors provide support service even to Free users.

Here are some general features of software vendor support system

- **Offline Support:** Offline support means the solution provided to the users queries through SMS, email, WhatsApp message etc.
- **Chain Support:** In case of complex issues, where deeper study and probe is needed to resolve the user problem, normally a ticket with unique Ticket ID is issued for the problem. Solutions are provided with reference to the Ticket ID, until the issue is resolved and Ticket is closed. The user gets the complete trail of the communication relating to the issue (ticket).
- **AI Chatbots:** Now-a-days Ai chatbots are ubiquitous in Support channels, for general Questions and assistance. Some systems provide smart chatbots which answers complex users queries almost like human. However, unless properly trained with adequate data, the AI chatbots may be pretty annoying.

- **Live Chat:** AI Chatbots provide machine assisted answers, to simple standard queries only. In Live chat, user types query or problem and a competent support service person instantly answers at the other end. The conversation goes on, till terminated by either side.
- **Phone Support:** This is the most commonly used support service. Like chat, in which conversations are in written typed words, phone support is through voice.
- **Live Support:** Now a days, both the user and the support service provider may share their computer screen real time. The user may show the problem live in their computer, and the service provider may access the user computer and resolve the problem, as if the support person is physically present on the users desk. This makes service efficient and instant, across geographical boundaries.
- **User Forum:** Vendor may provide user forums in which anyone may raise a query or problem in a public platform. It is reviewed and solution suggested by forum participants. This is very effective means to collaborate with users and resolve various kinds of user problems and experiences.
- **Complaints and Redressal:** Ultimately, there must be complain redressal means available to users if their problems are not resolved to their satisfaction. This is normally handled by an expert committee. It is an effective way to instill confidence among users and get their problems resolved.

Data Security & User Access

- **User Access Controls:** Role-based access for inputting, modifying, and viewing data, ensuring secure access.
- **Data Backup & Restore:** Scheduled and on-demand backups for local or cloud storage, with restoration options.
- **Data Import/Export:** Seamless data import/export with customizable formats (CSV, Excel, XML).
- **Audit Trail:** Tracking user actions with pre- and post-change logs.

Accounting Data Import & Export and Interoperability

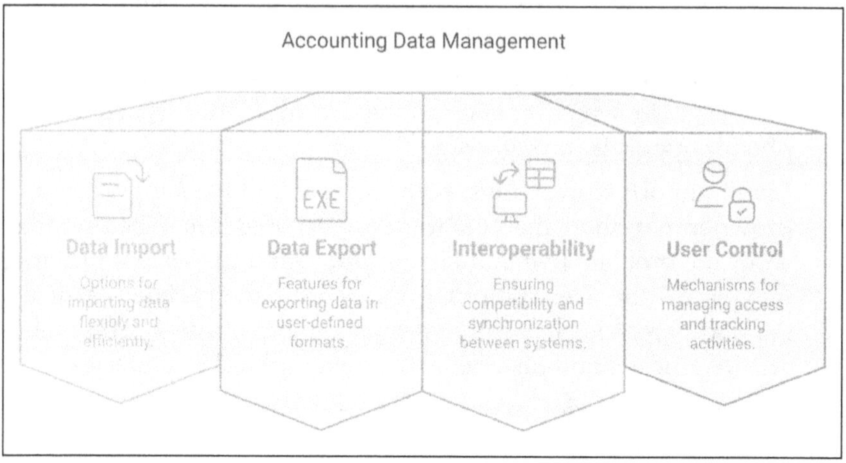

- **Data Import**
  - **Flexible Import Options:** Allow importing data from various file formats, such as CSV, XML, or Excel, to ensure compatibility with multiple systems.
  - **Customisable Data Mapping:** Provide tools to map import data fields to the system's database structure for seamless integration.
  - **Error Handling During Import:** Mechanisms to identify and flag errors in data during import for corrections.
- **Data Export**
  - **Export in Multiple Formats:** Support exporting data in common formats like CSV, XML, Excel, or JSON for use in other systems.
  - **User-Defined Export Templates:** Creation of user specified templates to export only relevant fields.
  - **Automated Export Features:** Scheduled or automated exports to integrate with other systems without manual intervention.
- **Interoperability between divergent systems**
  - **Data Compatibility:** Exported data to maintain its structure and accuracy when used in different software applications.
  - **Real-Time Synchronization:** Enable real-time data updates between integrated systems for consistency and reliability.

  - **Integration with APIs:** Support API connections to facilitate smooth communication and data sharing between systems.
- **User Control & Security**
  - **Access Controls:** Implement user-based permissions for importing/exporting data to ensure security.
  - **Activity Logs:** Maintain logs of data import/export activities for tracking and compliance.
- **Practical Use Cases:** Examples include transferring client records, synchronizing inventory between ERP systems, or exporting sales data to analytics tools for insights.

Software Customisation

- **Barcode/QR Code Integration:** Generation and printing for stock items, documents, and labels.
- **Customisable Dashboard:** A real-time overview of key data, with drill-down capabilities for detailed insights.
- **Report Accessibility and Sharing**
  - **Printing and Softcopy Saving:** Enable instant hardcopy printing and softcopy saving in PDF or Excel formats.
  - **Sharing Options:** Allow quick sharing of reports via email or other digital means with clients or external agencies.
- **Specialized Modules:** Optional features tailored to specific industries, trades, or business structures.

Data Connectivity & Information Communication

- **Automated Messaging:** Workflow-based automated notifications for updates and task reminders.
- **Mobile Access:** Data input, reports, info retrievals, messaging, directly from mobile / Tablet.
- **Messaging Tools:** Direct messaging to clients or team members via email or WhatsApp.
- **Banking Integration:** Secure online transactions and auto-bank reconciliation with major banks.
- **Cloud Storage:** Storage for all input and output documents on cloud drives, for any time/ anywhere sharing.

On-Premises Software Installation

- **Installation Process:** For On-Premises Software, Installation files are typically downloaded from the vendor's website for setup. The process must be smooth and straightforward, even for non-technical users. Clear and continuous guidelines should be displayed during installation to avoid errors.
- **Uninstallation & Reinstallation:** Simple process to uninstall and reinstall the software if issues arise or when transferring to a new computer. Proper explanation of the steps for uninstallation and reinstallation must be explained to avoid data loss or errors.
- **User Support:** A step-by-step installation guide and troubleshooting manual should be provided for user. Vendors should provide technical support or customer service for resolving installation issues.
- **System Requirements:** Ensure the software is compatible with the user's operating system and meets hardware specifications. Notify users of any prerequisite of Operating System, other software, hardware or related environment required for installation or upgrades.
- **Data Safety:** Backup existing data before reinstallation to prevent loss during the process. Recommend using an automated backup solution to protect critical information during updates or reinstallation.
- **Maintenance and Updates:** Provide regular updates to improve performance and address security vulnerabilities. Allow users to easily upgrade to newer versions without a complex installation process.

Data Input and Reports Output Customisation

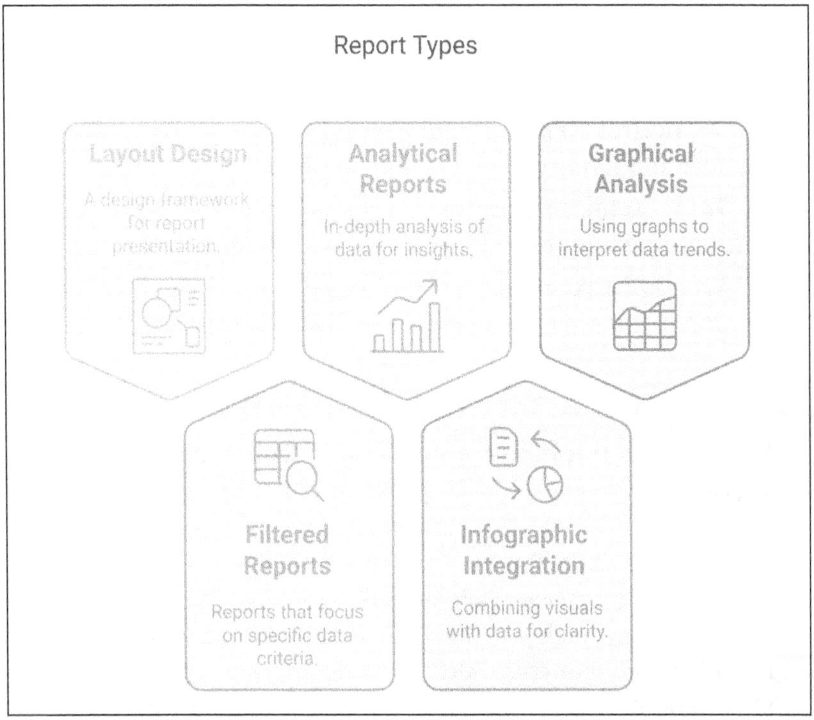

- **Customisation of Inputs Forms and Input Data Structure**
  - **User-Defined Data Fields:** Adding custom fields in master and transaction records to tailor the system to specific business needs.
  - **Flexible Data Structures:** Modify forms and inputs to capture additional information relevant to operations.
- **Customisation of Output Reports Layout and Contents**
  - **Standard Report Templates:** Templates for common reports to save time and ensure consistency.
  - **Document Designing:** Tools for Customising documents like invoices, incorporating brand logos, terms, or promotional content, such as showcasing best-sellers.
  - **Output Formats:** Outputs in multiple formats (e.g., PDF, Excel) for versatile sharing and storage.

- **Report Customisation**
  - **Report Layout Design:** Re arranging, realigning labels, data elements, totals & subtotals, infographics in user-defined formats.
  - **Filtered Reports:** Defining filters, conditions, and ranges to generate targeted and relevant reports.
  - **Analytical Reports:** Summarized reports using user-defined formulas and rules to aid decision-making.
  - **Infographic Integration:** To present data through visuals for intuitive understanding and impactful presentations.
  - **Graphical Analysis:** Generate graphs in diverse styles, with zoom and scale features for detailed analysis.

Messaging and Notifications

- **Workflow Notifications:** Automatically send updates to concerned user as per roles, as tasks progress through each stage of the workflow. Notify users about task completion, pending activities, and the next steps to ensure smooth operations.
- **Data Update Alerts:** Deliver real-time messages about critical data changes, such as financial updates, invoice generation, or inventory adjustments. Alerts should be clear about the current status and promptly reach the relevant team members.
- **Communication Channels:** Utilize popular messaging systems like SMS, WhatsApp, or email for reliable and instant notifications. Provide Customisation options to opt for preferred messaging platforms.
- **Task Reminders:** Set automated reminders for upcoming deadlines, such as payment dues, report submissions, or compliance requirements, ensuring timely follow-ups.
- **Security and Privacy:** Ensure messages contain only relevant and non-sensitive information to protect data confidentiality. Sensitive messages should be encrypted through secure transmission protocols.
- **Customization & Scalability:** Users may define messaging templates, priorities, and frequency based on their specific needs. The messaging system should be scalable as the organization grows or workflows evolve.

Operations through Devices

- **Remote Access:** Access information and reports remotely through mobile devices for convenience and quick decision-making. View real-time updates on financial data, inventory status, and transaction details while away from the office.
- **Mobile Data Entry:** Input data remotely, like customer inquiries, sales orders, Materials Delivery, Materials Receipts, etc, directly from a mobile device. Ensure verification and authentication of such Mobile data and seamless integration of authenticated mobile-entered data with the main system.
- **Task Management:** Enable employees to manage tasks on the go. Facilitate quick updates and responses.
- **User-Friendly Interfaces:** Intuitive and responsive mobile interfaces optimised for smaller screens. Simple navigation for report viewing and data input for non-technical users.
- **Security Measures:** Mobile operations are protected with encryption, secure logins, and access control mechanisms. Multi-factor authentication to safeguard sensitive data.
- **Customisation:** Customization of mobile functionalities based on user roles and business requirements. Offer offline modes to input data, syncing with the system when connectivity is restored.

Bar Code/QR Code Integration

- **Instant Scanning:** Integrate barcode scanners for instant and accurate scanning during data input, improving efficiency. Reduce manual entry errors by automating data capture through barcode scanning.
- **Smartphone Integration:** Integrate smartphones to function as Barcode / QR Code scanners, eliminating the need for dedicated barcode reading devices.
- **Barcode/QR Code Printing:** Print Barcodes / QR codes on invoices, labels, reports etc. Enhance document organization and inventory tracking with custom barcode printing.
- **Streamlined Workflow:** Integrate processes like inventory management, order fulfillment, and stock reconciliation using barcode integration. Compatibility with various barcode standards for versatile operations.

- **Customizable Features:** User-defined barcode formats and layouts tailored to specific business needs. Adaptation for operations like, retail, logistics, manufacturing etc.
- **Integration & Support:** Simple setup and integration of barcode systems with existing accounting software. Through intuitive interfaces and necessary user support.

Central Dashboard & Navigation

- **Centralized Overview:** Centralized dashboard displaying real-time snapshot of key performance indicators and business metrics, critical management information and actionable insights, at a glance.
- **Drill-Down Capability:** Drill down into detailed information directly from any dashboard element, for deeper analysis and quick decision-making by navigating from summary to specific data.
- **Customizable Dashboards:** Configuration of multiple dashboard formats to suit user preferences and business needs, allowing users to customise contents, highlighting key data and reports.
- **Quick Action Landing Page:** Configure dashboard as landing page for immediate access to frequently used features and actions, streamlined navigation to quickly reach critical functions.
- **Enhanced User Experience:** User-friendly interface with intuitive navigation and clear visual representation. Improves efficiency by consolidating essential tools and data in one central location.
- **Flexibility and Adaptability:** Adapting to diverse business requirements, supporting dynamic updates to the dashboard elements. Integrate with other software modules for a unified management system.

Audit Trail

- **Data & Operations History Trails:** Audit trail provides stepwise tracing history of all actions that modify approved and saved data, ensuring data integrity by recording changes to trace all subsequent updates.
- **Change Recording:** Tracks details of every change, including the user ID of the person making the change, the authority ordering it, and the date and time of the action, to maintain transparency and accountability.

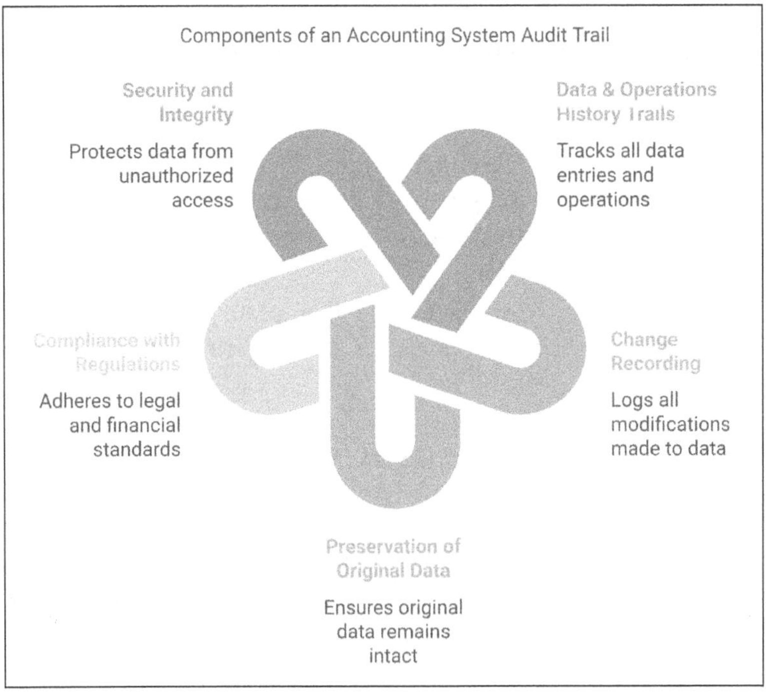

- **Preservation of Original Data:** Tags and preserves data before changes or deletions for future reference. Retain original pre-modification for further audits.
- **Compliance with Regulations:** Adheres to statutory rules and regulatory requirements for maintaining audit trails, maintaining legally compliant records.
- **Security and Integrity:** Prevents unauthorized data alterations by locking approved and saved records. Maintaining data security through tamper-proof history of changes. Support investigative processes through complete log of activities.

On-Line Banking through Accounting Software

- **Integration with Banking Systems:** Secure access to bank accounts directly from within the accounting software, eliminating switching between banking platforms and accounting tools.
- **Transaction Management:** Execution of banking transactions, like transfers, payments etc., within the software. Automated real time sync of accounting records showing transaction details.

- **Bank Statement Retrieval:** Enables direct retrieval of bank statements from the bank's site through the software. Saves time and reduces errors associated with manual downloads and data entry.
- **Automatic Bank Reconciliation:** Provides automated bank reconciliation, matching bank statements with accounting records. Ensures accurate tracking of account balances and identifies discrepancies promptly.
- **Secured Data Connectivity:** Complete foolproof secured connections to banking systems to prevent manipulations and fraud.

Cloud Drive Integration of Accounting System

- **Instant Uploading:** Automated upload of documents and reports to the cloud drive for secure storage. Eliminates the need for printing, reducing paper usage and storage costs.
- **Access from Anywhere:** Access to stored documents and reports from any internet-connected device, including desktops, tablets, and smartphones, from any place, any time.
- **On-Demand Printing:** Reports and documents can be printed directly from the cloud drive without accessing the accounting software. Simplifies the process of retrieving and sharing documents as needed.
- **Secure Storage:** Data security with password-protected cloud storage, for security and privacy.
- **Collaboration and Sharing:** Allows authorized users to view or share reports and documents remotely, improving collaboration. Streamlines communication between teams and external stakeholders.
- **Efficiency and Reliability:** Centralized storage and access to Documents and Reports. Easier and reliable backup and disaster recovery.

Industry focused Accounting Systems

Apart from general accounting systems as offered, many software provide separate customized modules for specific industry trade. Such modules are helpful for specific Industry, as they come with useful pre-configured features attuned to the specific business model.

CHAPTER 4

Business Accounting Software System Implementation

We have discussed various important aspects and features of Accounting Software; guidelines for review, evaluation metrics and selection process of the right accounting system as per organisation needs.

Classification of Business Accounting System

To make the review and evaluation process simpler and focused, we classify the popular Indian Accounting Software into following broad categories:

- **Enterprise Accounting System:** Covering all major functional areas of business, in a distributed system. These are targeted for large organisation for complete business information, Planning and Control.
- **Integrated Accounting System:** Covering various functional areas of Business, providing Business Information integrating all functional areas. These are targeted for Mid size organisation covering major areas of Business Functions.

- **Invoicing & Basic Accounting System:** Covering Quick Invoicing, Book Keeping and Basic Accounting Reports. These are targeted for Retail Invoicing & Accounting.

Every organisation intending to introduce computerized a system needs to make elaborate and extensive pre plan. In practice, following situations may emerge.

- First-time introduction of a computerized accounting system.
- Transition from popular apps like spreadsheets, to a computerized accounting system.
- Migrating from an existing computerized accounting system to a new system.

In any case, a pre- plan must be prepared, as explained in earlier chapter.

Accounting Software System Installation

Having selected the Accounting System, it is time to install the system in the organisation, depending on the type of software selected.

- **In-Premise System:** Installation process of on premises software will depend on the software. each software has their own installation process.
- **Cloud-Based system:** You don't have to install the software because this software is already on cloud. You have to login and register your name to use it.

In-Premise Software System Installation

In case of In-premises, normally you have to download an Installation wizard from the vendor's website, and then install in your computer in the specified place. During Installation, you have to provide various information. See the vendor's documentation for installation the process. Some software installation require technical knowledge and expertise. Take assistance of vendor to install the software in your computer correctly. This is a very crucial stage. The software may not work properly for any mistake or improper procedure

To get on hand help and assistance in installation from vendor or expert, it would be useful to install a screen sharing software, like TeamViewer,

AnyDesk, UltraViewer etc., in your computer, so that the vendor can directly access your computer and help you to install properly. Install the same software that the vendor is using or recommending. Such screensharing software will also be useful to get on-line dedicated support by vendor, from their own place, accessing your computer (they don't have to come to you). This is the usual dedicated support service method provided by vendors, now a days.

Software system Installation Issues

As explained, Installation may be complex and technical for some software.

- **Self Installation:** Check that you can do it yourselves. An online help and support should be instantly accessible throughout the System Installation process.
- **Vendor Assisted Installation:** In some cases, you need assistance of Vendor. See that all processes are user friendly and support is provided by Software Vendor in time.
- **Software Updates:** Be well conversant and aware of the rules and process of Uninstallation, Re-installation, License Update, Software Upgrades. Check up the vendor policy and user documents. Some vendors require special process / permission to change the key data of Company Profile, like Company name, Registered Mobile Number etc., change of server / device, moving the data to another device/ system, etc. Take note of these important issues.

Software Post Installation Work

- **Data Base Set up:** After installation, create and set up the database to store user created data structured manner. Some software first creates a central database. Some systems separate database for each business.
- **Company Profiles Creation:** The Company Data sets are normally created when you create the company (organisation) profile providing the required details of the company.

  So, First the software system database gets created. The organisation (Company) Data sets for each Company, are created next, as needed.
- **Initial data Preparation:** Having created the Company Data Base for a specific Company, first step is to collect initial data (Company

Profile and Masters data) from various scattered resources and entered into the system, through:

- o On line data entry into the system
- o Offline data entry outside the system

Company profile data may be quickly entered through software provided input form. Masters data may be input directly into the system or imported through various alternative method, as explained next.

Financial Accounts – General Ledger System Module

Financial Accounting Module covering the General Ledger System is the core module of Accounting System, which must be installed first, irrespective of other functional modules being integrated. A separate data sets would be created for each Company. So, we discuss General Ledger System as essential part of Software implementation.

- **Masters Data Entry:** After creation of company profile, create Masters data for the respective functionality. Masters Data may be entered directly through the application, or imported off line, as explained next.
- **Model Chart of Accounts:** Organise the Master Data into Multi Level hierarchal format, as per Accepted Accounting System. Almost all software provide Model Chart of Accounts to create organised Chart of Accounts, easily and quickly.
- **User Defined Input Data:** Apart from the standard data fields provided in the input form for Master entry, the software may provide for creation of its own additional elements, like, Numeric or text data fields, radio buttons, drop down list, muti line text box, multi select, Auto generated number, Attachment, validation rules etc., for each data Item, to customize the input data form.
- **Input Form Interface:** The Form layout aesthetics and organisation is important for data entry convenience. Similar info should be clubbed together. Information should be organised into sections.

The input fields should be logically organized. The input data should be instantly validated to prevent wrong data input. Selection options like drop-down list, radio buttons, checklists, etc, should be well organized, properly placed and intuitive. Normally a micro help of the currently focused option is displayed explaining a short description of the option.

General Ledger Accounts Masters

First the general ledger account Masters are to be created. In the same way the other Master's records are to be are also to be created.

- **Unique Master record:** Masters records are unique. To keep the sanctity and integrity of the system, two records of same Master should not be created. Each Master record is given a unique ID identifying the Master record. But sometimes, a master may have multiple unique IDs, and same master record may be identified or selected through any of the parallel IDs. A master record may be identified by unique name, numerical or Alpha alphanumerical code or mnemonics.
- **Hierarchal Structuring & Restructuring:** The masters should be properly linked to the parent master record to create ideal hierarchal structure. The structure of chart of accounts maybe dynamically changed and reorganized seamlessly, by moving a master from one parent to another.
- **Multiple IDs:** Normally, a master is uniquely identified by unique name, but sometimes a master may also be identified by multiple alternate unique names.
- **Opening Balance:** At the start of Financial Year account, the closing balance of previous Financial year is carried into current year.
    - **Entry in Specific Master:** In some system, the previous year closing balance is entered /carried as current year opening balance. In such case, each set of Master relates the specific financial year.
    - **Entry as first Transaction:** Alternatively, opening balance is separately entered in a special voucher as a transaction.

The later method may be better, the opening balance is de-linked from the master record. So, the master record becomes independent of financial year. Same Master may be shared between different financial year, and even between different companies having similar Accounting structure.

Masters Data Preparation Methods

First, we discuss about entry of masters Data entry to be done first. The Pros and Cons of Data Entry Methods in these two plans are discussed and compared.

Manual Master Data Entry into the system

- **One Shot Data Entry into the System:** The Data entry form in the software is pre-designed. You may enter the data through the software Data Input Form.
- **Piecemeal Data Entry into the System:** However, input data might not be organized in the same way as per the System Form layout and sequence. The input info may be scattered in various places. So, you may need to enter pieces of data elements (or related data items) from different sources.

For example, while entering customer profile data, you may need to input various detailed particulars that may be sourced from multiple locations. For example, the mailing address may be found in one area, while phone numbers and other contact details are located elsewhere, and tax information may be in yet another location.

The process of entering such dispersed data into a system's input form can present challenges. It requires opening the entry form, searching for and selecting the customer, and systematically filling in the relevant information in several steps. This necessitates selecting each customer and entering the pertinent data in smaller, organized sections. Consequently, this process can be time-consuming, particularly when dealing with large volumes of data.

- **Data Checking:** Having entered the data, it must be thoroughly checked for correctness.
- **On screen Checking:** Data may be checked on screen and mistakes rectified. However, on -screen checking and editing may be difficult for large volume data from entered from multiple input sources.
- **Data Checklist:** So, instead of Data checking directly on the entry form, you may need to print a checklist, to check the correctness and completeness of the entire entered.

You should make the Data Checklist Items conveniently aligned with input documents. You may need a program to print all the data elements on a single sheet, according to the input documents. The software may not offer such functionality to print data in a customized way.

So, Direct Data entry of massive data directly in system, though looks simple and straight forward, is often practically difficult. It is advisable to discuss the initial data input plan with your software vendor. You may also seek their assistance in getting the Master data correctly.

Offline Data Entry Outside the System

Instead of direct entry of Master Data, Data can be entered offline using popular applications (like spreadsheets) in a specified format, and then imported into the system using the data import tool. This is particularly useful for voluminous data, gathered from scattered sources.

We now discus the various methods and options of Off line data entry into the Accounting system, just before the start of Implementation.

- **Data Input Templates:** To make offline data entry, you may use a data entry template (for example a spreadsheet), as per aligned with input Form. Off line data input templates offer a simple and easy tool to import data into the live system. This may be done in two ways:
    - User Created template.
    - Using developer created template

We now discuss both the methods:

- **User created Data Template:** Looking at the data to be entered, the input form provided by the system, and data to be collected from various sources, you should design a template to conveniently collect all data in simplest and quickest way.
- **Vendor supported Data Template:** Often vendor provide the template into which data to be entered. Normally, vendor also provides a Data Import tool, to import data from such template into the system.

Data Capture into Input Templates

Having created a Template or selected the Vendor supplied Template, enter complete data offline into the Template Form. No info left out. Manually, check each data element carefully from the authentic input source. Instead of checking on screen, better print entire data sheet on paper. Check and mark the editing to be done. Edit the data. Now Off-line data entry is complete. Next step is to import the data into the system.

Data Import from Template into Accounting System

Depending on Template used, data may be imported from Template to System in two ways:

- **Data Mapping and Import:** In case of user created Template, map each data element of the offline system, to the respective data element in the software system, so that the data from offline system gets into the computer system properly.

Importing data to sofware system may sometimes be difficult, if the data structure is complex, or the data dictionary of the system is not properly and adequately documented. Proper data mapping may often require technical expertise. For small volume data, it may not be practically viable.

- **Through Data Import Tool:** Compatible data import tool to import the data from the template directly into the system, are often provided. They also provide data validation tool is to check the correctness, completeness, and integrity of the imported data.

Digital Data Migration

We have discussed Initial Data preparation through on line and off line methods. However, many organizations maintain important information in digital formats like MS Word, Excel, or other systems. Much of the initial master data may already be available in these digital applications. In such case, instead of manually typing the data into the system, options for data copying or migration should be explored. It saves significant time and ensures correct data entry eliminating manual typo errors.

Existing data in digital form may be migrated into live system by following methods:

- **Copy Paste:** Simple and non technical method is to copy data from exiting digital resource and paste into the entry form of the system. This is alternate to typing, but may result better quality data than manual entry, due to elimination of typo mistakes. The points discussed about One shot entry and piecemeal entry as discussed earlier, should be kept in mind.
- **Data Migration Tool:** In case of heavy volume exiting data migration situation, possibility of creating Data migration tool, as explained in Off line Data entry method, may be explored, In

such case, the migrated Data should be validated through a Data Validation tool to ensure data completeness, correctness and Integrity.

Disclaimer

We have compiled the information of few popular accounting software mainly from vendors' websites and documents, for general information of readers. We have not tested or worked with them, and do not guarantee or vouch for the performance of any feature or suitability of any products. Users should check the information with the vendor/developer, work with trial modules offered, check the support services, vendor reputation, etc., before making any decision.

Accounting System Implementation Plan – Key Takeaways

We have discussed challenges and issues of implementing a Computerised Accounting System, requiring meticulous planning. We have also discussed the initial data preparation plan and methods, the first step of implementing Accounting system. We again summarise key points of all the steps and tasks involved.

Accounting Systems Types

- **On-Premises Software:** Installed locally on company computers with full control over data but limited remote access.
- **Cloud Software:** Software and data reside on cloud server of the service provider, accessible via the internet, offering scalability and easier remote access, with updates and backups handled by the provider.

Accounting Data Base

- **Software Data Base:** After installation of In Premises Accounting Software, first the software data base is created to store all user created data.
- **Company Data Sets:** The software user may maintain Accounts of Multiple organisation (Company), spanning over multiple Financial Year Accounting period. After creation of Software data base, separate data sets are created for each such Company.

Data collection and Initial Data Entry Modes

- **Direct Data Entry:** Manual entry directly into pre-designed software forms. However, often it can be difficult for scattered data sources and voluminous data.
- **Offline Data Entry:** Data can be entered offline into a template form and imported into the system through proper impot tools. It is more suitable for entry from multiple data sources and large volume data.

Offline Data Input through Templates: For offline data entry, proper templates need to be created. Create your own template or use one provided by the developer. Enter Data into the Template Form, print for verification and edit to make data correct and error free.

- **Pre-created Templates:** Import Data from Template into the system, using the developer's import tool.
- **User Created Templates:** Map corresponding Data Items in the Template with the Application. Then migrate data. Validate Data for correctness, completeness and data Integrity.
- **Data capture Templates:** This involves filling out a structured template and importing the data into the system.
- **Data Mapping and Import:** It involves aligning fields in your existing data sources (e.g., customer names, Postal address, Phone Number,) with the corresponding fields in the Accounting system. For instance, ensuring that "Customer Name" in your spreadsheet matches "Customer Name" in system's database.
- **Data Migration:** Once mapping is complete, data can be transferred from the external source to the new system using a data migration program. It Helps automate bulk data entry instantly and correctly.
- **Validation of Migrated Data:** After data migration, it is essential to validate the transferred data to ensure
    - **Correctness:** The data is accurate and matches the original source.
    - **Completeness:** All relevant data fields have been imported without missing any critical information.
    - **Integrity:** The structure of the data remains intact without any missing link or corruption during transfer.

Data Validation is Critical to ensure the system functions smoothly

Transfer of Digital data from Other Systems

Many organizations already have master data in digital form, like Spreadsheet, other accounting software, etc.

- **Copy Paste:** Copy Data from the external digital media and paste into the System input form. It is simple, non technical, but time consuming.
- **Data Migration:** Map data between external system and the Application and migrate through a Data Migration tool. Validate Data for correctness, completeness and data Integrity, as explained.

Migrating from an existing to a new computerized accounting system:

- **In Built Migration Tool:** Many software systems provide tools to migrate from one system to another, like from Tally to their system, or from their system to Tally.
- **Data Export and Import:** In absence of In Bult migration tool between the two systems, first export data from the old system using its data export tool. Then Import the exported Data to the new System through Data mapping and Data Import Tool. For this you need to properly map data and create Data Migration tool to Import the data into the new system, validate the data for correctness, completeness and data Integrity. It may require technical expertise.

If data of both systems are incompatible and data migration is not practically possible, then type or copy paste into the new system, from the exported data of the old system. It is time consuming job for large volume data.

Financial Accounting Module – General ledger System

After creation of Company data set. For a specific Company, the Masters Data for core Financial Accounting Module covering the General Ledger System is created. There are several methods of creation of such data, like:

- **Direct Data Entry:** Manual entry directly into pre-designed software forms.

- **Offline Data Entry:** Data can entered offline, through model Pre created or user designed templates, as explained.
- **Data Migration form other applications:** Data existing in other application, may be imported through Data Migration tool or other suitable methods, as explained. The organisation may select the right method suitable for them

In the same way, data may be entered for other optional modules, or imported through Off line methods.

CHAPTER 5
Enterprise Accounting System

An enterprise system connects various modules for functionalities. A business has to manage three key resources (called 3M) - Money, Materials, and Manpower. A control module integrates all these functionalities in a centralized place, connecting data from all the modules and functions. Accordingly, we broadly divide the modules as per the management of these 3 resources, as follows:

- Financial Accounting - To manage Money
- Inventory - To manage Materials
- Payroll - To manage Manpower

What is an Enterprise Accounting System

Enterprise Accounting System is a general term loosely used to describe Integrated Accounting software systems, encompassing multiple functional modules of Business Accounting and management. These systems integrates functional modules to provide a holistic view of Business Functions, facilitating effective management and informed decision-making. However, the range and depth of functionalities can differ significantly among these software systems.

To focus on capabilities of such software systems, in this section, we define the Enterprise Application System (EAS) as those systems that extend beyond mere data aggregation from various activities. An EAS not only consolidates information but also prioritizes proactive management and forward-thinking decision-making by utilizing historical data to forecast and effectively manage desired outcomes.

This discussion will focus on the common features typically expected in an EAS. The deliberations aim to assist management in understanding the significance and coverage of evaluating the appropriate EAS for the business based on their specific requirements.

For the purpose of our discussion, we classify the functionalities of Enterprise Accounting systems into 3 major modules, for management of key resources, as described earlier, viz, Financial Accounting - To manage Money, Inventory Accounting - To Manage Materials Payroll Accounting - To manage Manpower and Tax Accounting to manage Tax Compliance - connected with all these three modules. We briefly describe each of them.

Financial Accounting Module

The following are key features of Financial Accounting module of popular Cloud based Enterprise Accounting System for large and medium scale Enterprises. These systems aim to integrate various business Accounting functions, of branches, works and offices, including work flow management, and instant sharing with stakeholders and targeted recipients.

Chart of Accounts Customization

To Provide a robust framework for accurate and scalable financial Information organization and reporting.

- **Multi-Level Chart of Accounts:** Flexible and pre-configured account structures suitable for various industries and business forms.
- **Sub-Accounts and Account Tagging:** Enables detailed classification and hierarchical representation of financial data for better granularity.
- **Bulk Updates and Base Currency Adjustments:** Simplifies account management across multi-branch and multi-currency operations.

Voucher Management and Transaction Processing

To Streamline transaction processing, ensure compliance, and maintain operational efficiency.

- **Categorized Voucher Entry:** Entries are validated based on transaction nature and accounting rules. Includes configurable replication and predefined narrations.
- **GST and Tax Compliance:** Automated GST postings for sales, purchases, and returns; includes TDS setup, deduction, and filing processes.
- **Multi-Level Approval Workflow:** Enables hierarchical approvals for all accounting vouchers, ensuring transparency and control.

Budgeting and Financial Controls

To Facilitate proactive financial planning, control, and performance monitoring.

- **Cost Center and Profit Center Management:** Enables tagging of transactions with cost elements for detailed financial analysis.
- **Budgeting and Budget Revisions:** Configurable budget tracking at ledger and cost center levels, with variance analysis for financial monitoring.
- **Transaction Locking and Recurring Journals:** Locks critical transactions post-approval and automates recurring entries for efficiency.

Audit and Financial Reconciliation

To Ensure accountability, compliance, and reciprocated compatibility of financial operations and records.

- **Audit Trail of Transactions:** Tracks changes in all documents, including user IDs, timestamps, and approvals.
- **Bank Reconciliation:** Automated reconciliation with configurable formats like Excel for ease of use.
- **Year-End Closing Entries:** Automates posting of closing entries, ensuring a seamless transition to the new financial year.

Reporting and Dashboards

To Enable informed decision-making with real-time and customizable financial insights.

- **Configurable Financial Reports:** Includes profit and loss statements, balance sheets, cash flow, and fund flow reports tailored to user needs.
- **Cost and Analytical Reports:** Offers multi-level cost reports and profitability analysis with graphical summaries.
- **Real-Time Dashboards:** Displays consolidated financial metrics with drill-down capabilities for granular details.

Petty Cash and Postdated Cheques Management

To Enhance cash flow management and ensure proper documentation of minor transactions, in a separate books.

- **Petty Cash Tracking:** Simplifies small cash transactions and tracks expenses accurately.
- **Postdated Cheque Management:** Ensures proper tracking and realization of future-dated payments.

Integration and Workflow Automation

To Integrate accounting with other business functions for a unified operational flow.

- **Inventory and Financial Linkage:** Automatic posting of accounting entries from transaction form other functional areas.
- **Workflow Automation:** Includes recurring journals, template-based journal entries, and cost center linking for seamless operations.

Materials Accounting Module

Materials accounting modules of Enterprise accounting systems, provide end-to-end solutions for managing materials, procurement, inventory, manufacturing, Job & Contract Work, Supply Chain Management, CRM, e-commerce and regulatory compliance, through integration across multiple locations and business functions.

Materials Procurement and Purchase Management

To Ensure timely procurement, maintain quality standards, and optimize procurement costs.

- **Purchase Order Planning and Management:** Supports purchase planning based on sales orders, manufacturing plans, and internal department requisitions. Includes auto-replenishment, vendor price comparisons, and purchase order tracking through vendor portals.
- **Goods Receipt and Quality Inspection:** Tracks goods receipt notes, enables customizable inspection parameters, and handles rejected goods via debit notes or replacements.
- **Cost and Expense Allocation:** Allows entry of additional expenses (transportation, customs duties, etc.) and includes landed cost computation for accurate purchase costing.

Inventory and Stock Management

To Optimize inventory control and reduce wastage while ensuring adequate stock levels.

- **Comprehensive Stock Tracking:** Multi-level inventory hierarchy, real-time stock levels, reorder points, and barcodes for stock Items, batch tracking with manufacturing and expiry dates.
- **Inventory Valuation and Methods:** FIFO, LIFO, weighted average, and standard valuation methods. Tracks inventory withdrawal and adjustments through physical stock verification.
- **Warehouse Management:** Automated stock allocation by bin and rack capacity, tracks goods in transit, and manages internal transfers between storage locations.

Manufacturing and Production Management

Production planning, quality control, improve production efficiencies.

- **Material Requirement Planning (MRP):** Raw material planning as per production schedules and multi-level Bills of Materials (BoM).

- **Production Processes:** Discrete, Process, Batch, and make-to-order manufacturing methods. Progressive bundling, line scheduling, and semi-finished goods tracking.
- **Quality Control and Waste Management:** Material testing, scrapping of unusable goods, waste reuse or disposal.
- **Cost Analysis:** Production costs computation, based on component consumption and BoM standards.

Sales Order and Distribution Management

Improve order fulfillment efficiency and customer satisfaction through optimum stock management and pricing flexibility.

- **Sales Order Processing:** Automated sales order creation, validation, and amendment. Bulk order creation, integration with B2B/B2C platforms, and API support.
- **Stock Reservation and Delivery:** Management of reserved stock, packing slips generation, multiple UoM conversions for deliveries.
- **Flexible Pricing and Promotions:** Customer-specific price lists, promotional schemes, approval workflows for discounts.

Supply Chain and Logistics

Supply chain operations for timely deliveries, facilitating logistics co-ordination.

- **Multi-Location Support:** Coordination across multiple branches, warehouses, and retail outlets with real-time stock transfer and tracking.
- **Rule-Based Replenishment:** Automated inventory replenishment based on sales patterns, seasonal demands, and predefined rules.
- **Goods in Transit:** Monitor shipments using RFID, mobile apps, and geolocation APIs.

Job Work & Contracts Management

To Enhance control over outsourced manufacturing processes and ensure accountability.

- **Outsourced and In-House Job Work:** Tracks materials issued to or received from job contractors. Tracking of stock consumption, returns, and work-in-progress management.
- **Job Contracts:** Manage contracts with principals, materials receipt, returns, and stock status with jobbers.

CRM and Sales Promotion

Strengthen customer relationships, drive repeat sales through personalized engagement.

- **Customer Relationship Management:** Track customer interactions, loyalty programs, and membership benefits across physical and online channels.
- **Sales Campaigns:** Targeted campaigns based on brand, category, and customer demographics with performance analysis tools.
- **Feedback and Surveys:** POS-integrated feedback collection and surveys.

Inventory and e-Commerce Integration

Expand sales channels, inventory synchronization across platforms.

- **Online Sales Integration:** Connect with e-commerce platforms (like Shopify, Amazon etc) for real-time stock updates and order management.
- **Automated Processes:** Auto-reserves stock for e-commerce orders and syncs invoices, shipping details, and payments with online platforms.

Reporting and Analytics

Deliver actionable insights for improved operational efficiency and strategic planning.

- **Inventory Reports:** Detailed stock ledgers, movement reports, and summaries.
- **Production and Material Reports:** Track Materials inputs, outputs, wastage, stock movements across processes.
- **CRM and Sales Reports:** Customer behavior analysis, loyalty program performance, and sales profitability.

Tax Accounts and Compliance

Compliance with GST regulations, better efficiency and correctness.

- **GST Integration:** Automated GST reconciliation, GST invoicing, e-way bill generation, e-invoicing, and GSTR filing (GSTR-1, GSTR-3B, GSTR-9, etc.),
- **Compliance Automation:** JSON-based e-filing, offline tools, and direct portal integration for tax filing.

Payroll Accounting Module

The payroll accounting module in enterprise systems provides a flexible and comprehensive solution to manage employee data, payroll calculations, compliance, and reporting. It enhances efficiency, ensures accuracy, and supports statutory obligations across diverse organizational setups.

Employee Information Management

Centralized employee information, streamline record-keeping across multiple locations.

- **Comprehensive Employee Database:** Maintain detailed employee records, including profiles, designations, work centers, and branch details.
- **Digital Documents:** Manage employee related documents and testimonials digitally for easy reference and compliance.

Pay Structure and Computation

Payroll computation for diverse employee categories and work conditions.

- **Configurable Pay Structures:** Define pay and deduction components, eligibility rules; salary structures for employees, groups, or designations.
- **Flexible Pay Periods:** User-defined pay periods (e.g Daily, Weekly, Monthly, Employee Specific) for different employee categories.
- **Computation Modes:** Computation based on fixed rates, attendance, time, or production-linked metrics.
- **Arrears Pay:** Compute and disburse arrears Pay with salaries or as separate payments.

Attendance and Time Management

Payroll processing through attendance, leave and other metrics.

- **Attendance Tracking:** Import attendance data from biometric devices, time sheets, or Excel files.
- **Time Logs and Analysis:** Record and analyze employee time in/out logs, overtime and under-time.
- **Leave Management:** Multiple leave types and rules (e.g., maternity, sickness, paid/unpaid leave) for employees or groups.

- **Holiday Setup:** Configure weekly, national, and festival holidays at employee, group, or company levels.
- **Production metrics:** Set Up Production metrics for computation of Production based Pay component.

Payroll Processing

Payroll processing with automated tools and customizable workflows.

- **Automated Payroll Calculations:** Payroll processing with configurable rules for pay, deductions, overtime, bonuses, etc.
- **Overtime Rules:** Rules and Rates for normal, weekly off, and Sunday overtime pay,
- **Pay Slip and Advice Generation:** Generate payslips, pay sheets, and bank salary advice for salary disbursement.

Statutory Compliance

Compliance with government regulations, reduce manual work, correct report filing.

- **Regulatory Reporting:** Generate and file statutory reports for PF, ESI, professional tax, pension.
- **I Tax Deduction on Salary:** Automated TDS on salary computation, Tax deductions, and filing of forms and returns.

Reporting and Analytics

Actionable insights, compliance reporting

- **Employee and Payroll Reports:** Generate Pay reports such as employee profiles, attendance, absenteeism, pay registers, and payroll analysis.
- **Customizable Filters:** Pay related Analytics, Customised reports through flexible filters for detailed insights.

Multi-Location Integration

Centralized payroll management for organizations with multiple work centers

- **Multi-Branch Support:** Payroll management across branches and geographical locations.
- **Production Integration:** Link pay with production metrics for performance-based calculations.

Popular Enterprise Accounting Systems

Brief details of following popular Enterprise Accounting Systems are described next.

- ALIGN BOOKS
- LOGIC SOFTWARE
- ZOHO BOOKS

ALIGN BOOKS

Align Books is Cloud based Enterprise Accounting System covering key areas of Accounting and Business Management, divided into functional modules. It also offers On-Premises module.

Sales / Billing

- **Orders & Deliveries:** Quotation & Estimates, Sales Order, Deliveries
- **Invoicing:** Similar / suggested products, Alternate UoM, multiple pricing, Invoice & Item level multiple discounts, free items
- **Invoice Printing & Sharing:** Printing & Saving Invoice in various digital format, sharing through email, WhatsApp etc.,
- **Automated Communication:** Auto notification of Invoice, Payment, Outstanding Dues.
- **Analytics:** Item wise Profitability, Customised Sales Report Analytics.

Purchase Management

- **Purchase Orders:** Purchase indents from internal departments, Stock Level based Auto Ordering for replacement, comparative pricing of vendors, past purchase history, Purchase Order creation, printing, & saving in digital format; Purchase Order sharing through multiple channels like email, WhatsApp and others,
- **Purchase Materials Receipt:** Materials acknowledgement, physical counting & measurement, quality inspection, rejection, debit notes and materials returns, receipt of accepted materials,
- **Purchase Invoice:** Invoice linking and data import from Suppliers Invoice, Landed cost computation for supplementary bills of Transportation, Customs Duty, Clearance Charges.

Financial Accounts

- **Configurable Chart of Accounts:** Pre-created flexible Model Accounts structure for various Business Form, Trade & Industry for customised Chart of Accounts.
- **Voucher:** Categorised Voucher Entry as per transaction nature and accounts rules validation; Voucher entry, Configured Voucher Replication from existing vouchers, Standard Voucher Narration, documents attachment in digital form.
- **Cost Centers / Attributes:** Multi level Cost Centres & Cost Groups. Linking of Cost Centre with each account transaction. Cost Reports. Cost analytical Reports and summary.
- **TDS:** TDS Set up, TDS rules set up, TDS in Party Master, TDS in Expense Master, TDS realisation from specified payment, TDS deposit, TDS returns, TDS Returns filing to portal.
- **Financial Controls:** Bank Reconciliation, Interest statements, Multi level work flow approval, Ledgerwise Financial Budgets, Cost Centre Budget, Budget revision, Budget Variations,
- **Financial Reports:** Fixed Assets & Depreciation statements, profit and loss account, Balance Sheet, Cash flow statements, Fund flow / Working Capital statements,

Inventory Management

- **Stock Item Masters:** Multilevel hierarchal Stock Item Groups, Categories & Stock Master, Item Serial No, Items classification through multiple attributes, Unique Barcode Generation, Barcode creation & map vendor barcode for each product, Multiple & Alternate Units,
- **Warehousing:** Organised Virtual & Physical Materials Storage Locations, Product/Item dimensions for storage capacity calculation, Storage dimensions for capacity calculation & Utilisation, Capacity management in terms of units and volume, Categorised Bin/Rack storage allocation,
- **Inventory Control:** Batch Numbers with Manufacturing & Expiry Dates, Expired/Damaged Stock/Inventory Management, Dead/ Slow Moving Stock Management, Bulk Package & Losse Inventory segregation, Inventory withdrawal method (FIFO, LIFO), Inventory valuation method (FIFO, LIFO, Weighted Average, Moving Weightage Average, Standard), Goods In Transit tracking & reconciliation across locations, Physical Verification & Auditing

of Inventory, Assembling/De-Assembling/Bundling of inventory, Materials Transfers,

POS

- **Stock Item Masters:** Multi Level Hierarchical Product Grouping, Parallel Categorization of Items, Definable Stock Item Attributes, Alternate & Compound UoM, Definable Custom Fields in Stock Items, Attribute Based Analysis, Minimum/Maximum, Re-order Stock level, Material Requisition, Serial Based Inventory ID, HSN/SAC Classification, Multiple Stores, Stores Stock consolidation, Inter Location Stock Movement,
- **PoS Transactions:** Similar / suggested products, Batch Number/Expiry Date, GST Compliant Invoice, Tax Inclusive/Exclusive option, Salesman wise Tracking, Invoice sharing with customer, Touch point PoS quick Invoicing, Pre set Price, Discount, Free items, Bundled Items, Bar Code scanner Integration, Multiple sales Counters, Home Delivery.
- **Invoice Payment Realisation:** Multi Mode Payments (Cash, credit card, PayTM, cheque, UPI etc), Cash Register Integration, Advance Orders management, Muti Campaign Sales Promotion schemes, Loyalty Cards, Loyalty Coupons, Rewards Points accumulation and Redemption, Cash Counter consolidation,

Job Work

- **Outsource Job Work:** Outsource Job Contracts with Jobbers, Bill of Materials, Materials Issue to Jobbers, Materials Receipt from Jobbers, Materials Returns from Jobbers, Materials Consumption & Standard variations, Stock with Jobbers,
- **In-house Job Contracts:** Job Contracts with Principals, Materials receipt from Principal, Job deliveries to Principals, Materials Returns to Principals, Materials belonging to Principals.

Production

- Semi processed materials Profile with ID & Bar Codes, Production Schedule, Production Process,
- Material Requirement planning, Multiple BOM, production & consumption voucher,
- Products Assembling, Dis-assembling,

- Unusable Materials, Wastage handling, re-use/ re process/ disposal,
- Materials Quality Control/Testing for Raw/Sem-Finished/ Finished Goods,
- BoM based Standard Product cost.
- Product cost for components / process/ Finished Items consumed,
- Work-In-Progress Management,

Payroll Accounting

- **Payroll Set Up:** Flexible Pay Periods, Employe Profile database, Employee Digital Documents attachment, Configurable Salary Structure, Pay & Deduction Heads, Computation of each Pay & Deduction elements, components calculations of dependent components.
- **Attendance & Leave:** Multiple Attendance & Leave Types, Definable Rules for Leave eligibility, Periodic Employee Attendance & Leave, Flexible employee level Duty In & Duty Out Times, Time In / Time Out records, Time machine Integration, Timesheet,
- **Payroll Processing & Reports:** Payroll Processing, Pay Slip, Paysheet, Bank Salary Advice, Employee Ledger, Payroll Statutory Reports (PF, ESI, P Tax, Pension, TDS etc) and filing to respective authorities,

Fixed Asset Accounting

- **Fixed Assets Profile:** Asset Acquisition, Asset ID, Asset Nature, Asset Location, Asset Supplier, Date of Purchase, Acquisition Cost, Fixed Asset Register,
- **Asset Maintenance:** Warranty & Maintenance Terms, Maintenance Schedule, Asset maintenance / repairs records, Maintenance Cost, Asset Upgrades, Expenses Capitalisation.
- **Asset Depreciation:** Depreciation Rate & Rules, periodical Depreciation Computation, Written Down Value,
- **Asset Disposal:** Asset Inspection, Asset Disposal / Transfer, Asset scrapping,

GST Accounting

- **GST Set Up:** Company GST Profile Set Up, Client GSTN Profile Set Up, Purchase Invoice, Sales Invoice / e-way Bill, Advance receipts from Customers/ Advance payments to Suppliers, Auto computed GST invoicing, automated e-way Bill Generation & Service Bills with HSN / SAC Code,

- **GST Filing:** GST Accounting, Periodical GST 2A / 2B Reconciliation, GSTR Payment, GST Portal off line & Direct Upload, GSTR -1, GSTR -3B and other GSTR Filing

Client Self Service Portal

Client Direct Login, Secured Customer/Vendor secured login, upload Quotations, view / download Purchase Orders, Purchase Invoice, Payments details, Ledger Books, Outstanding statements,

Align Books On Premises System

Align Books also offers Premises based system, on MS Access Database for Small Organisations, or MS SQL database, a Flexible & versatile system for Mid & large Organisations.

Align Books Pricing

- **Cloud System Modules:** Align Books is broadly classified into Basic, Premium, Ultima, and ERP modules, depending on functionalities. The license fees depend on functionalities used and data volume, as per charts provided in developer's website. The Certified Professionals module, with specified functionalities, is FREE for 3 years, while the Educational Module, with specified functionalities, is FREE.
- **On Premises Modules:** Single user: Rs 10,000, Multi user Single Location: Rs 25,000, Multi user Multi Location: Rs 50,000, Users need to pay one time fixed amount for Unlimited Volume, Unlimited Users & Companies.

LOGIC ERP

LOGIC ERP is Enterprise Accounting system covering all major areas of Business Accounting.

It is available as Cloud based SaaS (Software as a service), on a subscription-based model. It is also available as on-premises system for desktops.

LOGIC ERP comes with two main product ranges:

- A Complete ERP Solution as LOGIC Enterprise-Core, for large and medium enterprises
- Cloud (On-line) & On Premises (Off Line) modules, for medium and small enterprises

Logic Software is created on .NET framework. So, users need to install .NET framework on Windows (SQL Server database Engine & Management Studio) in their Server. They need to install Logic Software for Windows at Nodes. These require technical expertise.

Key Features

Materials Procurement Process

- Quotation and price comparison between vendors/suppliers
- Purchase Order planning based on Sales Orders/ Manufacturing plan, Inter Department Requisitions
- Auto-Replenishment Purchase Order, Standing Purchase Orders,
- Purchase order creation through sale orders for stock refilling
- Purchase order generation from Excel / External data through API
- Purchase Orders entry, amendment / history trail, Order Tracking
- Inwards goods acknowledgement, Inspection, Quality check with specified parameters
- Rejection / Replacement debit notes for rejected goods
- Goods Receipt Note for Accepted Goods
- Multi-level Approval for Vendor Payments
- Additional expenses entry, purchase landed cost
- Vendor Auto Service Portal,

Sales Orders Process

- Bulk sale order creation using Excel / Other Apps through API
- Sale Order creation converting buyers purchase orders
- Multi-level sale order approval / validation
- Packing Slip / Delivery Challan
- Delivery / Goods Transfers for Indents from retail stores/POS/ branches

- Job order creation through sale orders for production planning
- Sale order creation from Buyers Purchase Orders
- Sale Order amendment history, Sales Tracking
- Reserve stock against sale orders, Delivery Orders against reserved stock

Warehouse Management

- Hierarchal Physical & Virtual warehouse definition
- Item dimensions for storage capacity calculation
- Storage space dimensions for capacity calculation
- Storage Capacity as per units and volume
- Automatic bin wise stock allocation based on capacity calculation
- Internal storage stock transfer
- Physical stock verification through manual counting, RFID, Mobile app, PDA etc.
- Stock retrieval Bin Pick list

Manufacturing

- Material Requirement planning
- Discrete & Process manufacturing plan
- Make to order, Make to stock, Assemble to order, Make to assemble
- Batch manufacturing,
- Production Units, floor and line load and scheduling.
- Progressive bundling
- Range plan and sampling
- Multi-level Bill-of-Material
- Product / Package Marking, Barcoding.
- Materials Quality Control/Testing for Raw/Sem-Finished/ Finished Goods
- Scrapping of unusable goods
- Wastage handling, re-use/ re process/ disposal
- Product cost for components / process/ Finished Items consumed
- Standard Product cost based on Standard BoM.
- Work-In-Progress management

Supply Chain Management

- Multi-Branch, Multi-Warehouse, Multi-Retail/POS
- Rule based Auto-replenishment, Warehouse stock transfer
- Goods in transit Real Time Tracking
- Purchase planning from sale orders
- Retail store/POS refilling Plan
- Inventory re-filling Multiple parameters rules set up
- Substitution/alternate item/product suggestion
- Automatic re-filling of New items
- Seasonal Sales & Purchase planning
- Vendor portal Self Service
- Document work flow of Sale Orders, Delivery Orders, Sale Challans, Invoice, etc.
- Selling rate / Price List / MRP revision at Central Control Point / Retail Stores / PoS
- Sales/Goods return validation with Physical Verification, Rerun policy, Invoices, Damages, Expiry
- Multiple Sales price for Location, customer, customer group, product, markdown etc.

Invoicing

- User defined Invoice Format and Contents, Customisable Configuration
- Stock-in-hand verification during Order, Delivery Note / Invoice creation
- Instant Print, Save / Share in PDF / Excel, email / WhatsApp from Invoicing screen.

POS - Point of Sale

- POS system Configuration
- Touch/Mobile POS
- Flexible Schemes and promotions
- Weighing Scale Integration
- Multiple UoM Conversion
- Online ordering

- Home Delivery
- Cashier/Shift System
- Multiple Payment Modes, Payment Gateways
- Expiry Prompt

CRM / Loyalty

- Customisable Loyalty System for Points Accrual & Redemption
- Integration with third party Loyalty Programs (Banks, Credit Cards etc)
- Multi-Branch/Retail store wise customer management.
- Customer visibility across physical store, online website, omni-channel sales
- Brand/Category wise membership packages
- Birthday, Anniversary, Festival, Clearance Sales Discount and offers
- Discount Coupons and Gift Vouchers
- Discount Approval
- Customized On-line Feedback and Surveys, Feedback at POS

B2B Order Management

- B2B Platforms - Integrated, Cloud and Offline
- Product Catalogue with multiple images, Multiple views,
- Portal for Field Sales Agents/Salesmen order booking
- Portal for Customers for Direct Order Booking
- Portal for Customer / Agent for Bills tracking, Bills Outstanding, Payments Tracking.
- Portal for Field agents for work flow status updates
- Field agents Tracking through Maps / Geo-Location API
- Stock segregation by Design, Colour, Size and other attributes
- Multiple Items grouping for Order, Delivery
- Multiple orders auto generation from Pending Sales Order status
- Stock Validation of Orders, Order rejection / amendment for non availability
- Self Service Customer Portal, Vendors Portal

Inventory Management

- Multiple & Alternate Units
- Customized Barcode Generation scheme
- Expired/Damaged Stock/Inventory Management
- Bin/Rack wise Items
- Dead/Slow Moving, obsolete, defective Stock tracking
- Bulk Package & Loose Inventory segregation
- Product/item and Storage dimensions, storage capacity calculation
- Capacity management in units and volume
- Inventory withdrawal method (FIFO, LIFO and Actual)
- Inventory valuation method (FIFO, LIFO, Weighted Average, Moving Weightage Average, Standard).
- Goods In Transit tracking & reconciliation across locations
- Physical Verification & Auditing of Inventory
- Assembling/De-Assembling/Bundling of inventory

e-Commerce

- Item masters Share with B2C platforms
- Real time stock status with various B2C platforms
- Auto-receive orders from multiple B2C platforms.
- Auto-Reserve stock against orders received
- Multi-level approval system for sale order validation
- Delivery Orders against stock reserved
- Packing list creation,
- Order, Shipping, Invoice status sharing
- Schemes/discounts
- Accounts receivables/commission report sharing

Sales Promotion & Campaign

- Sales campaigns set up for Brands, Item Categories, Items, periods etc.
- Discount set up in percentage and value
- Sales Campaign set up for Retail Store/Branch/Branch Group
- Discount Coupons and Gift Vouchers schemes

- Pre-Paid Discount Cards
- Loyalty Discount Cards
- Points based accrual, redemption, and discount management
- Retail Customer Birthday/Anniversary Discounts
- Slow moving/dead stock Schemes/Discounts
- Manual Discount Entry approval
- Schemes and promotions Performance analysis

Payroll Accounting

- Employee Profile, documents & testimonials attachment
- User Defined Pay period for Employee Categories.
- Multi-Branch employee management.
- Pay & Deduction element computation,
- Pay / Deduction applicability rules set up at Employee, Group, Designation, shift or other user definable attributes.
- Fixed, attendance / time based, production based computation
- Configurable payroll computation rules for employee/ employee group
- Overtime and under time management
- Attendance data import from off line Excel Sheet, Attendance recording / biometric device
- Time in Time Out log & Time Analysis
- Multiple Leave Type / Leave Rules for Employee/ Group / Designation, maternity Leave
- Holiday Set up for Weekly, Festival, National, at Employee / Group / Company Level
- Normal Overtime, Weekly Off Overtime, Sunday Overtime rules
- Production linking with Employee / Team / Group
- Statutory reports (ESI, PF, Prof Tax, Pension, etc)
- Bonus Pay, Arrears Pay Computation
- Gratuity Computation & Payment
- Salary TDS Computation, deduction, TDS Forms, TDS Return filing.
- Pay reports like Pay Registers, Pay Slips, Paysheet analysis with flexible Filters and options.

GST Compliance

- Company GST Details
- GST Auto Computation in Sales Invoice,
- E-way Bill, e-Invoicing through GST Portal/ Excel / JSON
- GSTR-2A / 2B reconciliation
- GSTR-1, GSTR-3B, GSTR-4 & GSTR-9 generation
- GST returns e-filing

Accounts & Finance

- Multi Level Chart of Accounts
- Multi-Branch and Multi-Currency accounting
- Classified Voucher entry
- Cost Centers, Cost Elements and Profit Center tagging in Vouchers
- Cost Element Budget
- TDS Deduction, Payments, Reports Filing
- Sale/Sale Return Journal with GST liability posting
- Purchase/Purchase Return Journal, GST Input Tax credit
- Postdated cheque management
- Petty Cash management
- Multi-level approval and audit for accounting vouchers.
- Bank Reconciliation through excel
- Automatic posting of year end closing entries
- Accounts posting from inventory documents.
- Configurable reports and dashboards.
- Audit trail of all transaction & documents

MIS Reporting

- Report specific configurations for Data contents and filters
- Export of reports to excel spreadsheet
- Comparative analysis through multiple financial years
- User based data access roles
- Scheduled Reports generation, Report Auto mailing
- Mobile app for offline reporting

Reports:

- **Financial Reports:** Configurable DashBoard, P L Statement, Balance Sheets, Trial Balance, Financial Analysis
- **Sales:** Sales Order, Deliveries, Pending Sales Orders, Invoice, Invoice Books, Pending Invoices, Accounts Receivables, Age Analysis, Sale Registers, Sale Analysis,
- **Purchase:** Purchase Order, Pending Orders, Materials Receipts , Invoice, Pending Invoices, Accounts Receivables, Age Analysis, Sale Registers, Sale Analysis,
- **Inventory Reports:** Stock Items master details list, warehouse Stock reports, Stock Ledgers, Stock Summaries, Stock Movement Reports.
- **Production Reports:** Materials input to Process, Materials output from Process, Materials re-process, Materials Loss, Stock Transfers, Stock Loss / gains, Stock Adjustment, Physical Stock Verification & Adjustments,
- **Payroll Reports:** Employee Profile, Attendance / Work quantum, Leave / Absenteeism, Paysheets, Payslips, Pay Registers, Employee Ledger, Payroll Statutory Reports,
- **CRM Reports:** Customer Profile, Reward Points & Redemption,
- **User Access Reports:** User Rights Reports, User Logs

Logic On-Premises ERP

Logic On-premises ERP is also available. It is installed in User System, running on Windows 10/11 (32/64 Bit), without requiring Internet for regular work. However, Internet is required for Software Activation and Updates

Logic Software Pricing

Logic on-Cloud Pricing (Rs per month, ₹ 1100 exclusive of Taxes, Billed Annually)

- **Logic Business** – Selected Functionality offered in respective module
  - Basic - Starting at ₹ 1100
  - Standard Starting at ₹ 1188
  - Professional Starting at ₹ 1325

  - o Professional Plus Starting at ₹ 1512
  - o Ultimate Starting at ₹ 1900
- **Logic Enterprise** –All the Functionality offered
  - o Basic Starting at ₹ 6600

Logic On-Premise Pricing (Rs per month, exclusive of Taxes, Billed Annually)

- **Logic Business**
  - o Basic - Starting at ₹ 440
  - o Standard Starting at ₹ 553
  - o Professional Starting at ₹ 733
  - o Professional Plus Starting at ₹ 847
  - o Ultimate Starting at ₹ 1100
- **Logic Enterprise**
  - o Basic Starting at ₹ 4473

Prices vary according to features and functionalities used.

Logic Add-on-Modules

For on-Cloud, add on modules available at extra price:

- Payroll: Rs 1193 / month
- Production: Rs 1720 / month

and many others

Logic Mobile Apps

Additional Mobile Apps for Warehouse Management (Logic WMS), offline working and upload (Logic B2B), Customer feedback (Logic Feedback), On-line stores (Logic Aaptak), Delivery (Logic Delivery), etc., available.

ZOHO Books

ZOHO Books is a comprehensive Cloud Based accounting software, made in India, implemented world wide. It also offers a special India Specific simple module, complying to Indian Accounting Practice, and Tax Compliance, as described next.

ZOHO Books Features

Sales

- Sales Quotes, Sales Orders, Sales Approval
- Invoice customization, Invoice number multiple series, Recurring invoices, Multi-lingual invoicing, E-Way Bills, e-Invoicing, Credit Notes, Retainer invoicing
- Payment reminders, Online payments, On line payment links, Offline Payments
- Multicurrency invoicing & transactions, Automated exchange conversion,
- Customer Portal, Customer Management

Purchase

- Purchase Approvals, Purchase Orders,
- Materials Inward Acknowledgement, Inspection, Receipts,
- Purchase Bills, Purchase Expenses, Purchase landed costs, Recurring Purchase Bills & Expenses
- Vendor credits, Vendor Payments, Receipts Auto Scan & email forward,
- Multi-currency Purchase Bills & Transactions, Automated exchange conversion,
- Vendor portal, Vendor Management,

Banking

- Multiple bank / credit card accounts,
- Import bank/ credit card statements, Bank reconciliation
- Transaction rules
- Connected Banking with partner banks
- Setup bank & credit card feeds via third party provider

Financial Accounting

- Chart of accounts, Sub-accounts
- Journal templates, Journal Entries, Manual journals, Bulk Data Import
- Currency Conversion & adjustments

- Recurring journals, Transaction locking
- Budgeting, Cashflow forecasting

Inventory

- Stock Item Masters, Stock Levels, Price lists
- Stock tracking

Reporting

- Dashboard
- Report Exports in Spreadsheet, Excel, PDF,
- Reports Print, Reports Scheduling, Reporting tags
- Custom Reports

GST compliance

- GST Registration,
- GST Payments, GST Returns, GST Filing

Internal finance control

- Activity log
- Transaction locking, Record locking
- Custom user roles and access
- Transaction Validation rules & Approvals
- Digital Signature

Projects and Timesheets

- Projects Profiles, Project Budgeting
- Project expenses, Invoices, Retainer invoices
- Project tasks, Timesheet approval & and billing
- Project Profit Contribution

Customization and automation

- Invoice customization, Email template customization
- Custom reports, Custom views, Custom fields,
- Custom modules, Custom schedulers, Custom buttons and links
- Custom domain

Workflow Automation

- Workflow rules, Validation rules
- Email alerts, In-app notifications, Data updates
- Custom functions, Webhooks

Custom fields

- String: Single Line Text Box, Email, URL, Phone
- Numerical: Number, Date, and Date & Time
- Decimal: Decimal, Amount, and Percent
- Boolean: Check Box
- Multi Line Text box
- Lookup, Dropdown, Multi-select
- Number Auto-generate
- Formula
- Attachment

Document management

- Folders Creation
- Documents Upload
- Auto scan receipts
- Files attachment to Masters and Transactions
- Auto forward Documents, Bills, Receipts, Reports & Statements

Collaboration

- Customer & Vendor portal
- Comments
- Contextual chats
- Tasks Assignment and tracking

Advanced inventory

- Warehouse management
- Composite items
- Serial numbers & Batch tracking
- Bar Code labels, Shipping Labels,

- Shipments Tracking
- Online sales channels and Stores connection

Advanced Analytics

- Data visualization
- Custom dashboard charts and widgets
- Add and track customised KPIs and Formula
- External data collaboration for comparison & benchmarking
- Inter Department Collaborative reports
- Reports Embed in web sites/applications

Integrations

- Apps (Google Workspace, Microsoft 365, Dropbox, Google Drive, WhatsApp etc)
- Payment Gateways (Razorpay, Paytm etc)
- Banking (HDFC Bank, SBI etc)
- Zoho Apps (Zoho Payroll, Zoho Inventory etc)

Customer Support

- User Manuals, Blogs, Help Manuals,
- Email, Ticketing, Chat,
- Voice
- Device Sharing

Zoho Books Mobile Apps

Zoho Books Mobile Apps for Android & iOS, may be download Free of Cost from App stores & Play stores. registering through user's email id.

Zoho Books Mobile Apps - Key Features

- **General Ledger:** Recording of Transactions, maintenance of Books of Accounts and Financial Reports. Banking Transactions and Bank Reconciliation.
- **Client Profile:** Customers and vendors profile with Tax related info.

- **Sales & Purchase:** Sales Quotations, Purchase & Sales Orders, Materials Delivery Notes & Receipt Notes, Sales Invoice & Sales Returns adjustments, Purchase Invoice & Purchase Return Adjustments, Auto Reminders to customers for Due Bills Payments,
- **Customised Documents Formats:** Design Documents from in Built Standard Formats. On-line Payments to Clients and Vendors,
- **GST Accounting & Invoicing:** Maintain Company Profile for GST. Sales Invoice generation with auto computation of GST. E-way Bill, e-Invoicing for B2B transactions, Generation & Filing of GSTR-1, GSTR-3B, GSTR-4 & GSTR-9. Reconciles GSTR-2A, directly from ZOHO Books.
- **Inventory Accounting:** Stock Registers, Inventory Levels, Inventory valuation,

Zoho Books Indian Edition – Pricing

- Standard – Rs 799 – 3 users, email support,
- Professional – Rs 1499 – 5 users, e-mail and voice support
- Premium – Rs 2999 - 10 users, e-mail, voice and chat support

The above Rates are applicable for monthly billing, reduced rates for Annual Billing. Check the vendors site for current updates on features availability, threshold limits, etc, for respective plans.

FREE Module: Zoho also offers simple FREE module for Single User, covering Basic accounting, Accounts Receivables & payables, GST Accounting and Compliance, Customers and Vendors Tracking, Inventory Accounting & Control, with limited functionality. Users may upgrade to higher module later.

CHAPTER 6
Integrated Accounting System

The key features of an Integrated Accounting System for medium and small enterprises are now highlighted. They offer robust, scalable, and user-friendly financial accounting solutions that enhance operational efficiency and facilitate informed decision-making.

Financial Accounting Module

Core Financial Accounting Integration: To provide a unified system for managing diverse financial and operational activities efficiently.

- **Integrated System:** Combines financial accounting with invoicing, inventory, Tax Accounting, Manufacturing and Payroll, ensuring seamless synchronization between all modules.
- **Transaction Categorisation:** Enables systematic recording of transactions under predefined heads and Input document types, for accurate reporting and analysis.
- **Chart of Accounts:** Hierarchical, multi-level structures allow for detailed categorization of accounts and summarised reporting.

Accounts Management and Reports: To Facilitate effective monitoring, control, and analysis of financial health.

- **Accounts Master Setup:** Easy creation and configuration of company-specific account structures and vouchers.
- **Pre-Designed Templates:** Simplifies voucher entry and document preparation with customizable templates.
- **Books of Accounts:** Maintains ledgers, journals, summaries, and detailed account books for comprehensive financial management.
- **Accounts Receivables and Payables:** Tracks outstanding dues, bill-wise aging, reminders, and cash flow management for creditors and debtors.
- **Financial Statements and Reports:** Generates balance sheets, profit and loss statements, trial balances and other Financial Reports, in compliance with accounting standards.

Banking and Cash Management: To Ensure smooth banking operations and maintain liquidity transparency.

- **Bank Reconciliation:** Automates reconciliation with imported statements or manual entries for banking records.
- **Post-Dated Cheques Management:** Tracks and schedules PDCs for payments and cash planning.
- **Cash Flow and Funds Flow:** Forecasts cash positions, identifies surpluses and shortfalls, and generates actionable alerts.

Multi-Currency Support and Forex Management: To Support businesses operating in international markets with robust multi-currency functionalities.

- **Global Transactions:** Allows accounting and reporting in multiple currencies with real-time exchange rate adjustments.
- **Forex Gains and Losses:** Tracks currency fluctuations and incorporates them into accounts for accurate financial representation.

Budgeting and Financial Controls: To Strengthen financial planning and control mechanisms.

- **Project-Wise Categorisation:** Enables allocation of budgets and financial tracking at project or departmental levels.
- **Interest and Ratio Analysis:** Provides tools for interest calculations, profitability analysis, and financial ratios to evaluate performance.

Automation and Workflow Management: To Enhance efficiency and reduce manual effort in financial processes.

- **Payment Gateways Integration:** Supports automated payments and receipts processing through integrated gateways.
- **Workflow Automation:** Streamlines processes such as vendor payments, approvals, and reconciliations.

Comprehensive Reporting and Analysis: Provide actionable insights and enable communication of financial data to stakeholders.

- **Filtered and Configurable Reports:** Offers tailored financial reports such as cash flow, sales and purchase analysis, and profitability summaries.
- **Ageing Analysis:** Tracks overdue receivables and payables, aiding in timely actions for financial optimization.
- **Graphical and Shareable Reports:** Generates visual graphical charts for insights, Reports sharing in digital form and physical printing.

Compliance and Statutory Requirements: Ensure adherence to accounting and taxation standards.

- **Tax Accounting:** Automates GST and TDS compliance, including calculation, deduction, and filing of returns.
- **Depreciation and Regulatory Reports:** Generates compliant schedules for depreciation and other statutory financial documents.

Materials Accounting

Inventory Management

- **Stock Tracking:** Batch-wise stock management, stock valuation using multiple methods, tracking expiry dates for inventory items.
- **Multi-location Support:** Management of inventory across multiple warehouses, branches, or stores with real-time synchronization.
- **Item Categorization:** Organizing stock into hierarchical categories, groups, and attributes for better analysis and control.
- **Critical Stock Levels:** Setting minimum, maximum, and reorder levels with alerts for inventory replenishment.
- **Inventory Analysis:** Tools like ABC (value-based), XYZ (demand variability), VED (criticality), FSN (consumption rate), HML (price-based), and multi-criteria analysis.
- **Stock Aging and Reports:** FIFO-based aging reports and analysis of slow, fast, and non-moving items.

- **Inventory Valuation:** Multiple valuation methods such as LIFO, FIFO, and Weighted Average for financial reporting.

Inventory Masters

- **Stock Item Details:** Item master with HSN/SAC codes, GST rates, and detailed attributes (e.g., manufacturer, unit of measure).
- **Unit of Measure (UoM):** Support for simple, alternate, compound UoM, and inter-UoM conversions as per GST rules.
- **Batch Control:** Batch-wise inventory with tracking for manufacturing and expiry dates.
- **Substitute Items:** Managing alternatives for sales and purchase transactions.
- **Bundled Items:** Creation of combo Items and their components.

Inventory Vouchers and Transactions

- **Materials Movement:** Delivery notes, receipt notes, and linking with purchase or sales invoices.
- **Stock Adjustments:** Vouchers for losses, shortages, or adjustments.
- **Stock Returns:** Processes for sales and purchase returns, item replacements, and defective stock management.
- **Workflow Automation:** Wok flow transitions to next operation, like quotations to orders, delivery notes to invoices, accounts payables to Payment, etc.

Order Management

- **Sales and Purchase Orders:** Creation, tracking, and amendments of orders with pending order summaries.
- **Order Fulfillment:** Delivery schedules, anticipated shortages, and replenishment plans.

Sales & Invoicing

- **Customizable Invoices:** User-defined invoice formats with multi-currency support.
- **Pricing and Discounts:** Party-wise pricing, multiple price lists, date-based pricing, and discount schemes.
- **Tax Compliance:** Multi-rate GST, MRP-based billing, and automated tax calculations.

- **Point of Sale (POS):** Barcode and touch-based billing for retail environments.
- **Subscription Billing:** Automated invoices for subscription services with reminders for renewals.

Manufacturing

- **Bill of Materials (BOM):** Comprehensive BOM creation for production, including batch and process production.
- **Materials Issue and Receipt:** Tracking inputs and outputs during manufacturing processes.
- **Production Planning:** Tools for planning and managing production processes.

Inventory Reports

- **Stock Insights:** Reports on stock levels, expired items, stock value, and age.
- **Custom Analysis:** ABC, XYZ, and other inventory analyses for decision-making.
- **Warehouse-Specific Reports:** Detailed inventory and transaction reports by warehouse.

Customer and Vendor Management

- **CRM Features:** Tracking customer feedback, sales trends, Customer & Item order patterns.
- **Vendor Management:** Monitoring purchase orders, payments, and vendor performance.
- **Credit Management:** Setting credit limits and tracking overdue bills.

E-commerce and Integrations

- **Online Sales Integration:** E-commerce platform compatibility for inventory synchronisation.
- **Third-party Tools:** Barcode, weighing machine, loyalty management system integration.

Miscellaneous Features

- **Data Import/Export:** Importing data from supplier bills or other sources and exporting invoice data.
- **Reminders and Alerts:** Automated reminders for overdue payments, subscription renewals, and stock alerts.
- **Document Copying:** Quick creation of new documents by copying data from previous entries.

Payroll Accounting

Employee Information Management: Centralised employee information for efficient payroll and compliance management

- **Comprehensive Employee Database:** Detailed employee records, pay structures, positions, complete tenure history.
- **Digital Document Management:** Offer letters, employee documents, investment declarations, other records.
- **Employee Self-Service:** On line Employee access to pay slips, leave information, tax declarations, reimbursements, etc.

Pay Structure and Computation Rules: To Streamline payroll computations for accuracy and adaptability across diverse workforce needs.

- **Flexible Salary Structures:** Configure earnings and deduction elements for each employee, role, or branch.
- **Customizable Pay Heads:** Define and compute pay heads for allowances, deductions, taxes, bonuses, and variable pay.
- **Automated Salary Calculations:** Automate payroll processes, including attendance-based or time-based pay computations.
- **Promotion and Appraisal Management:** Record and implement changes in pay scales, designations, and increments.

Attendance and Leave Management: To Ensure accurate leave and attendance data integration for payroll processing.

- **Attendance Tracking:** Record daily or monthly attendance, including time sheets for project costing and profitability analysis.
- **Leave Management:** Define and manage leave types (e.g., paid, unpaid, maternity) and rules for eligibility and approvals.
- **Integration with Time Devices:** Import attendance data from biometric devices and time logs.

Payroll Processing and Disbursement: Simplify payroll processing and ensure timely disbursement.

- **Effortless Payroll Runs:** Calculate payroll and generate payslips in a few clicks, with detailed breakdowns of taxes, allowances, and deductions.
- **Direct Bank Transfers:** Process timely payments directly into employee bank accounts.
- **Loan and Advance Management:** Manage employee loans and advances, with adjustments reflected in payroll.

Statutory Compliance: Ensure statutory obligations compliance.

- **Regulatory Reporting:** Generate and file statutory reports, including PF, FP, ESI, TDS, P Tax, LWF, and I Tax.
- **Automated Tax Filings:** Handle employee tax filings and statutory compliance.
- **Online Return Filing:** File statutory returns directly through integrated portals.

Reporting and Analytics: To Provide actionable insights and simplify compliance tracking.

- **Comprehensive Pay Reports:** Generate reports like pay slips, pay registers, employee ledgers, compliance reports, and summary analytics.
- **Customisable Filters:** Analyze pay-related data using flexible filters and tailored views.

Integration with Accounting Systems: To Ensure integration between payroll and accounting modules for unified financial management.

- **Data Synchronisation:** Automatically post payroll amounts into respective general ledger accounts.
- **Branch-Wise Payroll Processing:** Manage and process payroll for multiple branches with consolidated reporting.
- **Easy Data Migration:** Import historical salary or previous employment data using pre-defined templates.

Employee Exit Management: Simplify and standardise employee offboarding processes.

- **Final Settlement Automation:** Process employee compensation and settlements automatically during exits.
- **Exit Documentation:** Send final settlement-related documents to employees' registered email addresses.

Popular Integrated Accounting Systems

Busy Accounting, Marg ERP, Profit Books, Real Books, Saral Accounts, Vyapar Accounting. Tally Prime

BUSY Accounting

Busy is On-premises Integrated Accounting system. A separate module to access and work on Cloud is also available. The key features are described below.

General Controls

- Multi-Company / Multi-Financial Year.
- Pre-defined Masters for Instant Start.
- Search, Sort, Filter and Group all Screen Reports
- Reports Export (Plain File / HTML / PDF / MS-Excel)
- Printing in DOS / Draft Mode
- Reports Drill Down to Voucher Level
- Print Preview
- Graphs and Charts
- User Definable Shortcuts / Favourites Menu
- User-Configurable Documents / Letters
- User-configurable Invoice / Documents / Letters.
- User-configurable Accounting Vouchers.
- Direct E-Mail / SMS
- MIS Reports & Analysis
- Customised Documents Formats / Alignment with Pre-Printed Stationery
- Data Checklist
- Import Vouchers from MS-Excel.
- Input Form Customisation
- Custom Validations in Masters / Vouchers
- Data exchange between BUSY and other Applications
- Document Printing in Standard Format

- User-definable Warning Alarms.
- Data Freezing.
- User Role based Access Rights.
- Back dated entries Controls (Full / Partial).
- Pop-up Calculator.
- Label Printing (Accounts / Items).
- Merging of Account / Item Masters.
- Voucher Replication / Duplication.
- Criterion based Query
- Multiple Criterion Report Filters
- Party Search by Name / Mobile / Email.
- Block / De-activate Accounts / Items.
- Import Masters from MS-Excel / Text File.
- Import Vouchers from MS-Excel.
- Images / Notes in Account / Item Masters
- Data Entry Forms Labels & Captions rename
- User-definable Columns in Reports
- Multi Language Invoice Printing
- User-configurable Invoice / Documents / Letters.
- User-configurable Accounting Voucher
- Voucher Audit
- Bind Data / User with Selective Computers
- Data Export / Import (XML)
- Direct E-mail / SMS to parties
- SQL Query Executor
- Notes / Task Manager
- Year-wise Data Back-up and Restore.
- Automatic Data Backup (Client-Server editions only)
- Collaboration tools to access Documents and Worksheets.
- Manual / Auto Data backup through Cloud, FTP, NAS Drives at data center.
- Data Migration from other Applications.

Financial Accounts

- Company Creation & Set Up
- Accounts Master Set Up and Creation
- Accounts Voucher set up and Creation, Voucher Statistics
- Multiple Voucher Series for each Voucher Type.
- User-definable Optional Fields in Masters / Vouchers.
- Voucher Entry / Edit during Reports Viewing
- Voucher Cancellation.
- Multi-Currency Financial Accounting
- Books of Accounts.
- Balance Sheet with various Schedules.
- Open Bills Reports (AR/AP), Age Analysis of AR/AP
- Daily / Monthly Summaries of Accounts / Groups.
- Bank Deposit Slip Printing.
- Configurable Payment Reminder Letters.
- Depreciation Chart (Books/ Income Tax).
- Interest Calculation / Posting in Accounts.
- Bank Re-conciliation.
- Accounts Registers with Configurable Columns.
- Post-dated Cheques (PDC) management.
- Configurable Balance Sheet & Profit / Loss A/c
- Multi-Currency Accounting
- Cost Centres
- Broker-wise Reporting
- Royalty Calculation
- Sub-Ledgers
- GSTR Reconciliation, error correction
- GST Register, GST Summary, Party wise / Itemwise; GST Returns Filing
- TDS Reports / Registers, Returns Filing
- TCS Reports / Registers, Returns Filing
- Cash Flow / Funds Flow.
- Ratio Analysis.

- Masters / Vouchers Statistics.
- Sales / Purchase Analysis.
  Profitability Reports (on various parameters)
- Branch Operation Offline & Online, Branch / HO Data Merging.
- Branch-wise Reporting.

Invoicing

- Sales / Purchase Order Processing,
- Sales / Purchase Returns, Replacement, Adjustment Debit Credit Notes,
- User-Configurable Invoicing
- E-way Bill Issue & Printing
- Multi Rate GST Invoicing (Local / Inter State).
- Tax Inclusive / MRP Billing.
- FREE Items / Free QTY in Invoice.
- Item / Party Past Invoice Price History during Invoicing.
- PoS Multi Mode Payment
- Sales Quotations / Purchase Enquiry / Purchase Indents
- Sales Order / Purchase Order.
- Delivery Challan / Sales Invoice
- Enquiry Management (from Receipt to Closure).
- Support Management, AMC tracking, Warranty Renewals

Inventory Control

- Multiple Warehouse
- Production / Bill of Material
- Inventory Masters, Multiple Price-List.
- Inventory Movement Vouchers,
- Multi Location Inventory.
- Stock Ledger, stock summary reports,
- Stock Valuation Methods.
- Critical Stock Levels
- Stock Ageing
- Primary, Alternate, Packaging Units,

- Batch / Mfg. / Expiry Date
- Item Serial Number,
- Item Attribute (Size, Colour etc.)
- Multiple Price-Lists, effective date
- Party-wise Price
- Item-Qty Discount Slabs
- BOM / Production Planning
- Production / Assemble / Unassemble
- Job work

Payroll

- Pay & Deduction Heads, Attendance & Leave Heads,
- Employee Pay Structure
- Employee Attendance & Leave
- Pay Computation,
- Statutory Reports
- Employee Loan / Advance.

Busy Mobile App: Mobile App for Android users to track accounting data on the go.

BUSY On -Premises Software Module Prices:

Perpetual License: (One Time Payment- Rs.)

- **Basic Module:** Single User: 9999, Multi User: 24999,
- **Standard Module:** Single User: 14999, Multi User: 39999,
- **Enterprise Module:** Single User: 19999, Multi User: 57999,

Subscription License: (Rs per Annum)

- **Blue Edition:** Single User: 5999, Multi User: 14999,
- **Saffron Edition:** Single User: 6999, Multi User: 17999,
- **Emerald Edition:** Single User: 9999, Multi User: 24999,

GST Extra as applicable

Busy Software On Cloud

Busy on Cloud is a SaaS solution in secured environment on internet connected device.

Busy on Cloud Price: Standard: Rs 800, **Business:** Rs 1000, **Enterprise:** Rs 1500 per month, Billed Annually.

MARG ERP

Marg ERP is On-Premises Accounting Software tailored to the Indian Business, offering specialized modules for small businesses, retail and distribution, with inventory-heavy operations. It covers areas of Financial Accounting, Inventory management, billing, GST filing, Payroll, and e-commerce integration.

Key features

System Controls

Company Creation: Company Creation & Company profile set up, Login & Password set up, Financial Year Set Up, Data Error checking and Repair, Back Up location set up, Financial Year Deletion, Switching between current and previous Financial Year. Data Restoration from Back Up. Cloud back Up, Data Auto Updation in Cloud Back Up.

User Role Set Up: User Set Up, Role Based Access Rights, Passwords,

Freezing of Data: Freezing of Specific Masters, Transaction Data upto specific date or Voucher Number in a Voucher Series, to restrict editing.

Internet access from within the Software: To collect info about Client, product, Tax etc, or any info from Internet, without closing or leaving the current working screen.

Highlight Notes: Rules for Coloured / Blinking info Transaction entry / Reports display in specific screens, for attention (like Credit limit exceeding, Expirable / Expired Items, Stock nearing minimum stock level, etc)

Inter Company messaging: Instant messaging among employees from the current working screen.

Data Import & Export: Export of Data in CSV, XML, XLS, DBF, format, and import from similar Format. Bulk Import of Off line Data in CSV & XLS files.

Messaging & email: WhatsApp / email messaging & message trails.

Mobile App Access: Access reports through mobile app.

Hot Keys: Hot keys, Exit key, Save, Apply, Cancel keys,

Menu option Search: Search option to locate the option in Menu.

Report Saving & Sharing: Digital media file saving and direct sharing through email, WhatsApp, SMS

Customisation of Input Forms and Output Reports: Customisation of Input Forms and Output Reports layout & contents, through User Defined Data elements creation.

Reports Printing: Reports printing on Printer, Reports saving in Digital Media (Excel / PDF), Cloud, Digital Reports / Cloud Links sharing in email, WhatsApp, and other messenger Apps,

Data Backup: Data Backup for Multiple Companies / Financial Years.

Financial Accounting

Chart of Accounts: Multi Level organised chart of Accounts creation under pre defined Account Groups and Sub Groups. Restructuring of Chart of Accounts.

Master Names in Regional Language: Translation / Input in regional language. Defining Local language and respective Fonts.

Accounts Masters: Masters Accounts creation with varied info according to nature of Accounts, Account Opening Balances entry,

Expenses Budget: Monthly Expenses Budget, Limit for Single Transaction or Total for Direct & Indirect Expenses, Account Groups and Accounts Ledgers, Budgets set up and revisions, Track Expenses and Budget vs Actuals variance, warning messages..

Voucher Series & Voucher Numbering: Creation of Voucher Series, Voucher Prefix, Voucher Suffix, Voucher Series initialisation period and date.

Voucher Number Sequence: Tracking of Missing Voucher Numbers, Duplicate Voucher Number, Back dated Voucher Insertion, Deletion & Cancellation.

Accounts Vouchers: Cash Vouchers, Journal Vouchers, Interest Vouchers,

Copying data from pervious Document: Data carrying from previous document for Quick entry.

Post Dated Cheques: Issue / Receipts of Post Dated Cheques, Reflection in A/R A/P reports, Post dated Cheques and maturity report. Bank Reconciliation of Post Dated Cheques,

Bank Reconciliation: Data retrieval from Bank Portal. Bank Reconciliation.

Accounts Books & Reports: Day Books, Accounts Ledgers, Transaction nature wise Ledger Books, Accounts Summary Reports and Analysis,

Financial Statements: Trial Balance, Profit Loss Account, Balance Sheet, Cash Flow, Funds Flow,

Fixed Asset Schedules: Assest Records with Depreciation Rules set up. Assets Register, Fixed Assets schedules with Original Value, Depreciation, Depreciated Value.

Payment Mode: Payment Mode set up for each Client, Multiple Payment mode,

Interest Computation: Ledgerwise Interest rate set up, Interest Computation, Interest Set up for each Bill Receivables, Due Date, Credit Days, Interest for delayed payment, Accrued Interest for Overdue Receivables, TDS Rate on Interest,

TDS: TDS Set Up, TDS Deduction, TDS payment, TDS Returns

Outstanding Reports: Accounts Receivable & Payables for Bill wise details, Age Analysis Slab set up, Slab wise Outstanding Reports, Age Analysis Summary,

Financial Analysis: Dash Board of key Financial Figures and Ratios,

Cash Flow: Operating Cash Flow, Investing Cash Flow, Financing Cash Flows.

Financial Year End Process: Closing of previous accounts, Previous Year Closing balances carrying to next Financial Year. Previous & New Financial year simultaneous operations. Locking of Previous year Accounts.

Inventory Accounting

Inventory Masters:

- **Store / Warehouse Master:** Multiple Stores. Virtual Multi Tier Stores organisation through Floors, BIN, Stores Blocking for Inventory verification.
- **Stock Item Master:** Complete Particulars of Item, manufacturer Master linking with the Stock Item, Storewise Stock Item Open Balance. Batch ID with Mfg & Expiry Dates
- **Unit of Measure:** Simple Unit of Measure, Alternate Unit of Measure, Compound Unit of Measure, UoM as per GST rules. Entry of UoM in transactions, Inter UoM Conversion,

- **HSN Master:** HSN / SAC Short Name with Codes (in 2,4,8 digits) for the Stock Items used, and linked with Stock Items. Details of GST Rates.
- **Bundled Items:** Bundled Items (Combo Items) and Components Masters.
- **Substitute Materials:** Items of same nature classification
- **Inventory Reports:** Inventory Levels Set Up, Inventory Valuation Methods set up for Stock Groups / Stock Items / Entire Inventory, Inventory Valuation Methods for Financial Reports, Inventory Valuation reports. Godown / Batch Stock reports, Expiry Date Stock Reports, Expirable Items Stock Reports, Ageing Stock Reports. Return of Expired / Defective Items to Supplier, Replacement of Expired / Returned Defective Items.

Sales

- **Salesman Master:** Creation of Salesmen and linking in Orders, Invoices, sales man wise detailed and analytic reports.
- **Area Master:** Areas of operation of Business, to get Areawise Sales analysis of salesmen.
- **Route Master:** Create Master to set the standard Route of movement of sales people for efficient marketing and receivables collection from Debtors.
- **Country Master:** Create list of countries, with Country Particulars, in which the organisation conducts business, to get Country wise Reports and Analysis
- **State Master:** Create list of States in which the organisation conducts business, to get Country wise Reports and Analysis.
- **Price List Master:** Party Categorisation for Price & Discount, Different set of Prices of Items, Item Prices for Parties, Datewise rate / Scheme, Free Item on Bill Value,
- **Discount Master:** Discount / Special rates for Parties / items, Maximum Discount set up in Item Master, Bill Value Slab / Discount Rate, Point System set up and Discount / Redemption of Points,
- **Sales Schemes Set Up:** Set up schemes rules and invoicing as per scheme rules,
- **Sale Boosters:** Stock Item tagging for Stock Clerance sale, New Item Launch, Special Scheme,

- **Credit Limit:** Credit Limit for Parties,
- **Reminder Set Up:** Auto Reminder set up for Due Date, Overdue Bills,
- **Masters Check List:** Master Check Lists in user defined format

Invoicing

Multiple Price and Discounts Lists, Cash Memo, Delivery Challans, Invoice, Sales Return & Replacement on Sale Bill, Salesman / Route / Area Wise Bills & Reports, Indication for Min, Max, New / Old Rate & Expiry, Previous bills history during Billing, PoS Invoicing, Import data from suppliers Bill

Subscription Billing: Auto created billing for subscription based services. Entry of subscribers, subscription receipts, renewals, tracking, reporting and management of Subscribers data.

Inventory Vouchers: Materials Delivery Notes, Materials Receipt Notes, Materials Sales Invoice, Materials Purchase Invoice, Linking of Materials Delivery & Receipt Notes with Materials Sales and Purchase Invoice, Purchase Materials Return Out, Sales materials Return In, Debit Notes and Credit notes for Retuned materials, Debit & Credit Notes for Rates and other Accounts Adjustments, Materials Shortages, Materials Losses, Materials Delivery Note / Packing Slip Printing. Stock Transfers,

Stock Returns: Return of Stock Items, Replacement of Returned Item.

Manufacturing

- **Manufacturing Process:** Manufacturing / processing of Items with Input and Output details. Stock adjustments of Consumed and Produced Items. Re processing of Items.
- **Bill of Materials:** Bill of Materials for Production Items, Issue of Input Materials and Production of Output Materials vouchers using Bill of Materials. Batch / Process Production, Materials uses variance for Batch Production.

WorkFlow set up: Stepwise work flow from Enquiry Quotation to fulfilment of Order, From Invoicing to complete accounts clearance, from materials issue to receipt of finished products through intermediate manufacturing stages.

CRM Features: Basic features of customer relationship management, like Customer Visits, Customer feedback, customer sales trends,

Itemwise sales tracking, order frequency chart, etc, Special offer of clearance sales of outdated, non moving old stock, expiring stocks,

Cash Discount: Cash Discounts schemes and accounting for early or timely payment.

GST

- **Company GST Set Up:** GST registration & related details se up for the Company
- **GST and Cess Rate set up:** Company Level, HSN/SAC Code, Item Level, Category Level, Stock Group level, GST Computation Basis (Ad valorem, Quantity, Price Slab), GST Nature (Non GST, Exempted, FREE Items),
- **Stock Item GST Details:** HSN/SAC Code, GST Rate.
- **GST Invoices & Billing:** GST Compliant Invoice Generation, Bar Code. Auto validation of Buyers / Suppliers GSTIN
- **E-Invoicing:** e-invoice authenticated by Invoice Registration Portal (IRP).
- **E-way bill:** Single, Multiple & Bulk e-way bill, directly upload on portal.
- **Party data Collaboration:** Data transfer between the vendor and customer through GSTIN / e-Code.
- **GST Reports:** GST related transactions Direct posting to GSTN portal in Excel, JSON or CSV Format.
- **GST Return Filing:** File GSTR 1, GSTR 2, GSTR 3B, GSTR 4, GSTR 9 directly from the software.
- **GSTR 2A Reconciliation:** GSTR-2A purchase bills auto download. GSTR 2A reconciliation.
- **GST Payment:** Input & output tax & RCM Adjustment. GST Payment.

TCS: TCS Set Up, TCS Billing, TCS payment, TCS Returns

Payroll Accounting

- **Employee Profile:** Employee Particulars, Departments, Designation, Pay Structure
- **Attendance & Leave:** Attendance, Leave, Overtime, Production,
- **Payroll Processing:** Auto computation of Pay / Deduction Heads, Posting to Financial Accounts.

- **Pay Reports:** Pay slips, Pay Registers, Pay Summary Reports, Employee Ledgers
- **Statutory Compliance:** Returns and Payment to respective Authorities, like Provident and Pension Fund, Professional Tax, ESI, LWF, Income Tax Deduction etc,.
- **Data Migration:** Export Reports to Excel / Other Applications, Import Attendance and other Data from external applications
- **Employee History & Positions:** Chronological record of changes in Employee profile for the entire employment tenure.
- **Employee Exit Management:** Final settlement of Pay, Bonus, Gratuity and other remuneration.

Marg ERP Software Modules Prices

Marg ERP Software is available in 3 different Features & Price Modules

- **Basic:** Rs. 9999 for 1 User Full Rights (₹ 3000 per extra user. Maximum 2 users, ₹ 3000 per extra Company. Maximum 2 Company), covering following functional & operational areas
- **Standard:** 12600 for 1 User Full Rights, 1 User for View (₹ 3000 per extra user ₹ 3000 per extra Company)
- **Gold:** Unlimited Users, Unlimited Companies.

PROFIT BOOKS

Profit Books is Cloud based Accounting software covering Financial Accounting, Invoicing & Inventory & Payroll. The key features are described next.

Key Features

General Controls

- **Company:** Company Profile, Company logo, Preferences Settings, Branches,
- **Devices Integration:** Multiple Platforms & Devices, Operating systems, Printing Devices, Scanning Devices, Cash Drawers,
- **Reports Printing & Sharing:** Hard copy Printing, saving & sharing in digital format,

- **Messaging & Communication:** Messaging, Report and information sharing like e-mail, SMS, WhatsApp, and other channels, directly from within the application through email
- **Users Access Controls:** Role based multiple users with specific access rights. Multiple Users, Role-based Access, Auditor Access

Financial Accounts

- **Financial Accounting:** Chart of Accounts, Project-wise Categorisation, Payment Gateway Integrations
- **Transaction Entries:** Transaction recording under accounting head & categorization for Proper Accounting Analysis and reporting.
- **Multiple Currency:** Accounting transactions in multiple currencies, Exchange Rate fluctuations, Forex gain Loss Accounting,
- **Banking:** Import Bank Statements, Auto & Manual Bank Reconciliation, Payments & Receipts through Payment Gateways.
- **Accounts Receivables:** Accounts Receivables Tracking, Due Date amendment, Receivables Schedules, Ageing Analysis,
- **Accounts Payables:** Accounts Payables Tracking, Due Date amendment, Payables Schedules, Ageing Analysis, Vendor Payment workflow from Accounts Payable,
- **Accounting Reports:** Accounts Books & Summaries, Ledger Accounts, Balance Sheet, Profit & Loss, Cashflow,
- **Audit Trail:** Trail of Records of masters & Voucher Alteration.
- **Tax Compliance:** Taxation Reports (TDS, GST, TCS)

Materials Purchase

- **Purchase:** Purchase Order, Pending Purchase Order Tracking, Purchase Order Amendment, Materials Receipt, Purchase Invoice linking to Purchase Order & Materials Receipt, Inwards Delivery Schedule, Purchase Invoice,
- **Vendor Management:** Track and manage vendor details, purchase orders, Materials Receipts, payment histories. timely payments, Email vendor statement, Convert Purchase Orders to Materials Receipts, Purchase Invoice,

Sales Management:

- **Sales Orders:** Sales Quotations to Anticipatory and Customer Enquiries, Sales Orders, Pending Sales Order, Delivery schedule, Orders amendment, Customer Advance,
- **Invoicing:** Customised Invoice Format and contents set up, Invoice Numbering scheme, Multi-currency Invoices, Sales Analytical reports for Sales Tracking. Payments links in the Invoice, Online Payments receipts from Debtors, Automated Reminders for Open Accounts, aging reports on outstanding dues.
- **Customer Management:** Customer Statement of Sales Order, Sales Invoice, Money receipts from Debtors, Workflow from Quotations to Orders to Materials Deliveries to sales Invoice to Accounts Receivables to Debtors Outstanding.

Inventory Management

- **Stock Items:** Stock Item organisation into hierarchical Stock groups & categories, Multi level Virtual & Physical Warehouse, Item Attributes, Item Batch Mfg. & Expiry dates, Alternate & Compound Unit of Measure, Minimum, Maximum, Re-Order Stock Levels,
- **Manufacturing:** Bill of Materials, Materials Issues to process, Materials Production from process, Stock Transfers,, Stock Losses & gains, Stock Adjustments,
- **Inventory Control:** Stock Reports, Stock Summary & Stock Analysis, ABC Stock Controls, Slow, Fast & Non Moving Items, Stock Scrapping & Disposal,

GST: GST Invoicing, e-way Bill.

Payroll Management

- **Payheads Setup:** Set up each employee pay Heads for earnings and deduction elements
- **Define salary structure:** Define Pay Structure of each employee with computation rules
- **Attendance & Variable Pay:** Recording of Attendance, Leave with Pay and Without Pay, and variable Pay details for each employee, for the respective Pay Period
- **Payroll Processing:** Calculate all Pay and Deduction heads amount for each employee for the respective Pay Period. The

amount of each pay head is posted into respective general Ledger Accounts.

Profit Books Pricing:

- **FREE Start Up Module:** Create professional invoices in multi-currency, track receivables, manage business expenses and get tax report- *Single User. Create Upto 25 Invoices Per Month, Manage Upto 100 Customers, Track Upto 25 Products or Services. Start for Free, upgrade to SMB later.* So, Start Up module is practically a FREE Trial module.
- **SMB Module:** All features - Rs 749 per month. *Supports Unlimited Users* with unlimited individual access, *Create Unlimited Invoices, Manage Unlimited* Customers, *Track Unlimited Products or Services.*

ProfitBooks Mobile App

ProfitBooks Mobile App for Android & iOS may be downloaded free. It does not collect or share any data with third Parties. The data is encrypted in transit. User may request the Data to be deleted.

Profit Books Remote Book Keeping Service

Profit Book helps Accounting Freelance Service to provide remote on line service to clients. Business organisation having small space and no spare technical person or expert Accountant may outsource the accounting process to freelance accountants.

- Business organisation will routinely enter/ upload the data and scanned documents on Cloud Google Drive) with secured access to Service Providers.
- Accounting Service Providers will download all data / documents through their secured access, capture the data in software, process the reports and store them in Cloud in organised manner
- Business organisation will view the reports, at any time, from any place, using any Internet connected device (Desktop, Laptop, Chromebook, Smartphone, Tablet, or other compatible device)

The service is FREE for one month.

REALBOOKS

RealBooks is a cloud based Accounting Software, with following key features

- **Brach Accounts Management:** Multiple Branches Accounting, Branch Integration, Real-time Branch data consolidation, Branch Reconciliation.
- **Data Import / Export:** Bulk import in predefined formats, raw bank statement uploads, customized Excel formats. data migration and export in Excel, PDF, CSV,
- **Management Reports:** Segment Analysis Report, Columnar Comparative Reports, Cashflow & Cost Center Report
- **Compliance Management:** Multiple GSTINs, TDS return Filing via excel and API, GST e-Way Bill / e-Invoice generation
- **Document Management:** Attach documents with masters & transactions, Unlimited Cloud Storage, Document Upload Report
- **Customer & Vendor Management:** Customised Bill Ageing Analysis, Due Bill notification, Customer Credit Limit & Credit Period, Bill Wise Status Tagging.
- **Banking:** Cheque auto-configuration, Cheque printing, bank integration payments, bank reconciliation.
- **Inventory Management:** Stock Aging, Valued Stock Report, Order Management, Multiple Pricelists
- **Accounting Reports:** Accounts Books, Sale & Purchase Reports, Financial Statements
- **Role-based User Access Control:** Role Based User Permission & Rights, Back-dated Operations Control, customizable approval hierarchies, workflow Notifications & Alerts.
- **Data Security:** Hosted on Amazon AWS Servers with Top Data Security, Bank grade 256 bit encryption, Multiple Levels Data Back Up.

Payroll Module: RealHR is a separate cloud-based Payroll Solution, integrated with Online Accounting Software

Mobile App: Access accounts on the go with Mobile App, for anywhere, anytime accounting.

RealBooks Pricing: Free 14 Day Trial, Professional – Rs 500 per month per user, Business: Rs 1000 per month per user, Enterprise: Rs 2000 per month per user

SARAL ACCOUNTS

Saral is On-premises Financial Accounting cum GST Compliant Invoicing Software. It does not offer any cloud or Mobile operation module.

Features

- **Financial Accounting:** Chart of Accounts, Accounts Vouchers, Accounts Reports), Voucher Entry Templates, Bank Reconciliation, Cheque Printing, Cheque Deposit Slip, Post dated Cheques,
- **Ordering,:** Purchase Order, Inward Materials Receipts, Rejection and Returns, Multiple Price Lists, Multiple Sales Discounts schemes,
- **GST:** GST Sales Invoicing, e-Invoicing, GST Purchase, GSTR 2A Reconciliation, Input Tax Credit, Reverse Charge Mechanism, E-Way Bill, GST Reports & Returns Filing.
- **Service Invoicing:** Multi level Service Job masters, Service Order, Multi-Service Invoice, Recurring Service Invoice, Reverse Charge Mechanism,
- **Invoicing:** TCS Invoicing, Sales Reports, Debit Credit Notes,
- **Inventory:** Stock Reports, Bar Codes,
- **PoS:** Customer Loyalty Points, Multiple Counter Billing,
- **TDS:** TDS Accounting, Reports, Return Filing
- **Warranty / AMC:** Warranty, AMC Management, AMC Auto Renewal
- **Other Features:** Group of Companies, Sales Scheme Management, SMS, WhatsApp, email Integration, User Security Control, Data Migration & Sync, Mobile Integration
- **Auditor Module:** Data Synchronisation with Audit System, Remote Audit Operation
- **Dashboard:** Central dashboard showing key financial position.

Modules & Pricing

- **Saral Bronze:** Price: 7500 for Single User, 15000 for Multiple User.
- **Saral Silver:** Price: 15000 for Single User, 20000 for Multiple User.
- **Saral Gold:** Price: 12000 for Single User, 25000 for Multiple User.
- **Saral Diamond:** Price: 25000 for Single User, 35000 for Multiple User.

Saral Business Modules: Saral provides following distinct set of functional Modules, separately priced.

- **Financial Accounts:** Comprising Saral Accounting , Saral Billing.
- **Payroll:** Saral paypack, Saral ePF ESI,
- **Tax and E Filing:** Saral RDS, Saral Tax Office, Saral Income Tax, Saral GST, Saral XBRL, Saral TDS Web, Saral FinTrac, Saral Sign

Saral Paypack: Saral Paypack is a separate Payroll Management software,

- **Employee Profile:** Employee profile, Increments, Promotions, for entire tenure period.
- **Pay Structure:** Pay & Deduction heads, computation rules.
- **Attendance and Leave management:** Attendance and the leave details of the employees.
- **Statutory Compliance:** All the statutory requirements like PF, ESI, PT, TDS, reports and online return filing to the respective portals.
- **Pay Reports:** Pay related reports like Pay Slip, Pay Registers, Employee pay ledgers and summary reports
- **Employee Self Service:** Employees can update leave information, reimbursement information, Tax related declaration, online.

VYAPAR ACCOUNTING

Vyapar is On-Premises Integrated Accounting Software providing following features and Functionalities

- **Chart of Accounts:** Hierarchical organised multi level structure of Chart of Accounts.
- **Accounts Transactions:** Data entry of regular transactions classified as per nature of transaction
- **Accounting Books Reports:** Journal Day Books, Accounts Ledgers, Accounts Summary Reports, Financial Reports, Financial Analysis Reports. Trial Balance
- **Accounts Books:** Accounts Ledgers, summaries & analysis, Trial balance
- **Financial Statements:** Profit Loss Statement, Balance Sheet, conforming to IAS (Indian Accounting standard).
- **Accounts Receivables & Payables:** Accounts Receivables & Payables Reports, Reminders for Due and Overdue Bills, Cash flow

of Payments and Receipts to Debtors / Creditors, Cash positions forecasts, Cash surplus and shortfalls triggers / alerts .

- **Multi-Currency:** Base and Foreign currency, currency exchange rates, Reports in Foreign and Base Currency, Forex gain Loss Accounting.
- **GST:** GST Set up, HSN/SAC code integration, Invoice generation, GST Reports and filing GST Statutory Returns.
- **TCS:** TCS Computation in Invoices, TCS Accounting and Statutory Reports complying to TCS Rules
- **TDS:** TDS Computation and Deductions, TDS Accounting and Statutory Reports complying to TDS Rules
- **Stock and Inventory:** Creation of Inventory Masters, Inventory Transactions, Stock Reports.
- **Order Management:** Purchase and Sales Orders, Orders fulfilment, Open Orders Management, Orders Modifications.
- **Data Import from Tally:** Data Import / Export To and from Tally
- **User Role Management:** Sets user access and operations rights to maintain responsibility and integrity of data.
- **Customised Documents Formats:** Pre created model invoice formats_for quick and easy design of Documents Formats and customisation as per needs and choice.
- **Collections Management:** Accounts receivables details, Analysis and control.
- **Revenue Maximisation:** Sales Forecast, sales analysis in various parameters, Sales boost and profit maximisation strategy.
- **Business Performance and Financial Health:** Track sales trends, cash flows, open orders, payment updates, due date reminders. Dash board to show the key info and action plans.
- **Updated Status:** current bank status, stock and inventory status, open orders, cash flow and other requirements online.
- **Online and Offline Access:** On line module also allows off line operations without Internet connection and auto update on Internet connection (useful in remote / weak Internet area).
- **Payment Options:** Integration with various Payment Gateways like UPI, QR, NEFT, IMPS, e-wallets and credit/debit cards etc, embed QR Code in Invoice
- **Data Backup:** Automated data backup on every data update instance. Additional Local Back Up

- **Brand Logo:** Logo maker to create business logo.
- **GST Compliance:** GST compliant Item HSN/ SAC code, e-way Bill, Delivery Notes, Invoice, e-Invoice, GST Returns (GSTR-1, GSTR-2, GSTR-3B, GSTR-9 and GSTR-4) filing, GST payments and upload on GST portal.
- **WhatsApp Integration:** Documents sharing, money transactions, messaging, chats, through WhatsApp. Integration with Business WhatsApp.
- **Role Based User Rights:** Users creation and Role based Access Rights.
- **Hardware Integrations:** Diverse hardware Integration like barcode scanners, QR Code scanners, Smartphone Bar Code and QR Code scanning Apps, thermal printers, cash drawers, multiple printers like DMP, Inkjet, laser Printers, through wire & remote connection. Operating system like Android, iOS, Windows, Mac, devices like SmartPhone, Tablets, Desktops, etc, Integration with various common software tools & utilities.
- **Godowns/Stores:** Physical and virtual organisation of multiple storage location, Materials movements and Inventory.
- **Inventory Management:** Consolidation of stock. Stock movement analysis, fast, slow & non moving Items, Inventory Analysis like ABC (based on Stock Value), XYZ (based on demand variability), VED (based on criticality to operations), FSN (based on consumption rate), HML (based on unit price), SDE (based on supply/ demand), and multi-criteria analysis (combining multiple factors e.g demand and value). Stock Levels like Minimum, Maximum, re order and alert set up for each level.
- **Automated Payroll Calculations:** Automated employee salary calculations, deductions, and other payroll-related tasks, through Vyapar›s payroll module.
- **Order Management:** Sales and Purchase Orders, Materials Arrival and Delivery schedules, Anticipated Shortages, Stock Outs, replenishment plan. Open Orders, Auto Reminders and messaging for pending deliveries.
- **Work Flow:** Document conversion workflow like, Payments for Accounts Payables, Receipts from Accounts Receivables, Sales Orders from Quotations, Purchase Orders from Indents, Stock status reports, sales Invoice from Sales Delivery Challans, Goods Receipt Notes from Purchase Orders, etc.,

Price- Silver – Rs 3239, Gold 3599 - per year for small users. Additional cost for Large User modules.

Vyapar Free App for Mobile

Vyapar app for Android devices, downloadable at Google Playstore, is free for a lifetime. Supports devices like Smartphone, Chromebook, Tablet.

- **Data Privacy:** Vyapar Mobile app may collect Personal info, Contacts and other info, App activity, Share App info, App activity & performance, and Device or other IDs with third parties. Data is encrypted in transit. User may request for Data to be Deleted.
- **Features:** It enables to Track Expenses, create Invoice, manage Online Store, maintain stock inventory, generate GST Reports, supports printing from Mobile.

In Free App, the Vyapar Logo is embedded. In premium version of App, the Vyapar Logo is removed, data may be synced in multiple devices (license to be bought for each device).

TALLY PRIME

Tally Accounting Software is recognized as one of the most established accounting solutions, boasting a substantial user base for nearly four decades. So, we delve into some more details into Tally, than other software discussed in previous sections, to provide more insights, for large current users and potential customers.

Over the past four decades, Tally has built a large user base. Its initial popularity among business communities can be attributed to innovative features tailored to the specific needs of Indian businessmen, which are often not addressed by other accounting software or textbooks.

Tally is an on-site integrated accounting system, that includes essential features such as financial accounts, invoicing, inventory control, GST compliance, and Payroll accounting, all in one package.

Overview of Tally Accounting System

In contrast to many other software solutions, that offer various versions with distinct pricing, Tally is presented as a comprehensive package encompassing all features and modules. It is available in both single-user (where only one user can operate at any given time) and multi-user (allowing multiple users to work simultaneously) configurations.

Tally Integrated Accounting System – Functional Areas

While Tally is offered as a unified package, it can be broadly categorized into several functional areas, including the core General Ledger System and optional modules such as accounts Receivables and Payables, Invoicing and Inventory, and Payroll Accounting. These functional areas can be activated or deactivated as needed, allowing users to customize the system to meet their specific requirements.

Core Controls

- **Multiple Companies:** Multiple Companies (Organisation Accounts) creation with general common set of Chart of Accounts, irrespective of organisation trade, or constitution.
- **Chart of Accounts:** All user created accounts must be organised under rigid structured Tally Pre configured Reserved Chart of Accounts (which cannot be restructured by user).
- **Defined Voucher Types:** Specified Voucher Types auto created by Tally, creation of peer voucher type, but new voucher type, with user defined criterion or rules, not allowed.
- **Dashboards:** Central Dashboard showing consolidated financial metrics with drill-down capabilities for granular details.
- **Accounts Inventory Integration:** Optional Stock value link of Financial Accounts with Inventory, or independent user specified stock value input.
- **Emails:**E-email set up and email of documents and report from with the system.
- **WhatsApp:** Conditional access to allow WhatsApp set up and sharing documents through WhatsApp,
- **Voucher Series & Voucher Numbering** ; User defined multiple Voucher Series, Voucher Prefix, Voucher Suffix, periodic number re-initialization. Duplicate Number, Number skipping and reuse, Automatic number re-sequencing, Back dated Voucher Insertion, Modification, Deletion & Cancellation. Back dated voucher entry controls.
- **Voucher Duplication:** Voucher Duplication for similar / repeating transaction.
- **Menu option Search:** Menu Option Search also by synonyms.

- **Reports Printing:** Reports printing on Printer, saving in Digital Media (Excel / PDF),
- **Data Import Export:** Data mapping tools to import from, and export to, external applications with diverse data formats,.
- **Data Management:** Data Back Up in user specified media, Data Restore, Auto Back Up in Server module only.
- **Role-based user rights:** Role based user rights set up at action level, through a complex interface.

Financial Accounting

- **Budgeting and Financial Controls:** Rudimentary Budget features to enter user specified Budget for Ledger Accounts, Account Groups and Cost Centres, Financial Projection (Scenario). No parametric formula or rules for Budget computation. Budget and actual variance reports.
- **Cost / Profit Center:** Multi Level Hierarchal Cost Centres and Cost Groups. Tagging of transactions with cost elements for Cost analysis reports.
- **Audit Trail:** Audit Trail report showing ID of altered transaction. Pre Alteration or Deleted records not preserved. Alteration reasons, approvals, notes not maintained to refer back for probe.
- **Financial Reports:** Profit and Loss statements, Balance Sheets
- **Currency:** Multiple Currency Set Up, Currency Conversion, Forex Gail Loss Accounting
- **Bank Reconciliation:** Data retrieval from Bank Portal. Auto & manual Bank Reconciliation.
- **Accounts Reports:** Day Books, Accounts Ledgers, ledger analysis, Accounts Summary Reports,
- **Financial Statements:** Trial Balance, Profit Loss Account, Balance Sheet,
- **Cash & Funds Flow**, Cash & Funds Flow reports showing Receipt/ Payment; Working Capital change; Operating Cash Flow, Investing Cash Flow, Financing Cash Flows not available.
- **Financial Analysis:** Dash Board of key Financial Figures, Key Performance Ratios,
- **Post Dated Cheques:** Issue / Receipts of Post Dated Cheques, Reflection of Post Dated Cheques in A/R A/P reports,

- **Interest Computation:** Ledgerwise / Billwise flexible Interest Rate, Interest Receivable & Payable,
- **Outstanding Reports:** Outstanding Reports of Receivable & Payables with Bill wise details, Age Analysis Slab set up, Slab wise Outstanding Reports, Age Analysis Summary,

Tax Accounting

- **TDS Accounting**
  - TDS Activation, Masters TDS set up, Vouchers, TDS Deposit, Statutory Returns
- **TCS Accounting**
  - TCS Activation, Masters TCS set up, Vouchers, TCS Invoice, TCS Deposit, Statutory Returns
- **GST Accounting**
  - GST Activation & Set Up, Regular & Composition Dealers,
  - GST Set Up for UoM Master, Stock Group, Stock Item,
  - GST Classification, HSN, Supplier & Customer,
  - Tax Invoice, Bill of Supply, e-way Bill,
  - Input Tax Credit, Reverse Charge,
  - GST Reconciliation, Issues & Troubleshooting
  - GST Payments & Accounts Adjustment
  - GSTN Portal Data Upload, GST Returns filing,

Materials Accounting

- Inventory Activation & Set up
- Inventory Masters, Godown, Batch,
- Orders, Orders Outstanding
- Materials Delivery & Receipt
- Sales & Purchase Vouchers, Invoicing,
- Physical Stock Adjustments,
- Inventory Reports
- Inventory Valuation
- Manufacturing, Assembling, Unassembling,
- Job Work In, Job Work Out,

Payroll Accounting

- Payroll Activation & Set Up
- Pay & Deduction Heads, Employee Master, Pay Structure
- Attendance, Production,
- Allowances & Deductions,
- Payslip, Pay Advice, Paysheet, Pay Registers, Pay Reports
- Bonus, Arrears, Overtime, Leave Pay, Gratuity,
- Payroll Statutory Reports
- Employee I Tax Liability / TDS Computation

Exclusive Features of Tally

Accounting System aims to generate accurate financial records while adhering to business practices and regulations. However, Tally distinguishes itself by offering unique features that enable creation of user curated accounts. Some of them are briefly pointed out for user information and awareness.

- **Post Modification:** Allows reconstruction of accounts through transaction modification dynamically from Reports, even after compiling final accounts, facilitating user curated accounts as desired.
- **Voucher Numbering:** Tally allows unusual methods like Voucher number skip, re-use, insertion, renumber etc, which may lead to manipulations.
- **Closing Stock Value:** Unlike traditional methods, Tally records Closing Stock Value on the fly, impacting Profit & Loss and Balance Sheets, to facilitate Accounts curation.
- **Stock Valuation Methods:** Stock Value can be manipulated by dynamically changing Valuation methods, without reporting deviations in valuation method.
- **Inventory Value:** Inventory value can be effected independently through Stock Journal entries without supporting accounting effects.
- **Data Hiding/Restoration:** Tally allows selective hiding of report items, leading to potentially misleading reports.
- **Physical Stock Voucher:** Users can adjust stock quantities without journal entries, affecting stock manipulation & stock valuation.

Tally intends to offer some unique features & flexibility, but these pose risks to integrity, ethics, and security in accounting practices.

Legacy Software System

Tally is legacy software System. The term "Legacy software" is used for "outdated computer systems, applications, or technologies, that are still in use". Legacy software is sometimes difficult to avoid and replace, because of its wide and long use. However, Legacy software is too slow, or too late to embrace benefits of changing new technology.

Due to technological limitations, essential features such as Workflow Automation, Graphs, Custom Fields in Forms and Reports, Document and Reports customization, etc. available for long, even in low-cost contemporary software, are still absent in Tally.

Limitations of Tally

- **Focus on Reporting:** Primarily generates accounting reports without actionable insights for business efficiency.
- **Graphs and Charts:** Lacks advanced graphical representations; only basic bar and line graphs available.
- **Column Sorting:** Limited sorting options; no multi-column sorting.
- **Checks and approvals:** Instant saving of voucher on entry, without checks and approvals stages. Lacks internal checks and controls.
- **Actionable Workflow:** Requires re-entry of data for related processes; no workflow synchronization to move to next stage document carrying data from previous stage. .
- **Notifications and Alerts:** Many critical deviations or exceptions not alerted during data input. Automated messaging or reminders lacking.
- **Input Forms:** Primitive design; cumbersome navigation and poor visibility; lacks customization options.
- **Budgets:** Manual Budget figures input. Dynamic user-defined parameters and computation rules not available, to compute or revise budgets.
- **Auto Data Backup:** Auto Back up available in Server module only.
- **Mobile Access:** Limited report retrieval capabilities.
- **Chart of Accounts:** No model charts for different trade / industries, legal structure. Pre defined rigid account structure.

- **Earnings Analysis:** No pre defined Account groups for Depreciation, Amortisation, Finance Charges, Interest, etc, to auto evaluate key earnings performance, like Pre depreciation Profit, OIBDA, EBT, EBIT, EBITDA, et al.
- **Voucher Controls:** No tools to track, control or identify missing, duplicate, or non sequential voucher numbers.
- **Pre-Edit Data:** Deleted data not retained; pre-edit data of edited records not traceable.
- **Customization:** Limited to predefined Configuration options; No custom templates, user defined fields for precise customisation of Input Forms, Documents & Reports, as desired by users.
- **Payment Modes:** No option for client specific pre defined multiple payment modes.
- **Report Saving:** Reports directed to printer by default. Instant saving in digital format (like PDF, XLS) are complicated.
- **PoS System:** Rudimentary PoS features. Lacks sales promotions, loyalty programs and other PoS features.
- **Manufacturing:** Very basic manufacturing journal, Bill of Materials. Process Master, Manufacturing Stage, inter-process transfers, and multi stage manufacture features are missing.
- **Fixed Asset Schedule:** Fixed asset schedule forming part of Balance sheet not generated. Inadequate fixed asset reporting; lacks detailed schedules of Assets acquisitions, disposal, depreciation details, Original Cost & WDV .
- **Chart of Accounts:** Deviates from standard structure in some respects, often requiring reorganization of Tally created Balance Sheets.

Price

- Single user (Silver Edition) 22500 one time license fee. Monthly rental 750 / month
- Multi user (Gold Edition): 67500 one time license fee. Monthly rental 2250 / month

Conclusion

The decision to implement a legacy system such as Tally, or to opt for a contemporary system as outlined in this book, is contingent upon the specific objectives of the organization. Tally is proficient in generating wide array of reports, derived from user input and historical accounting transaction data. However, it falls short in some critical areas, such as workflow automation, input forms, documents and reports customisation, business planning, budgeting, actionable reporting, alerts, sharing and communication of data and information.

If accounting is the primary concern, Tally may be a suitable option. Conversely, if the focus is on enhancing efficiency in business management, manufacturing capabilities with stage-wise process control, or robust internal security, coupled with streamlined workflow features, it may be prudent to consider other contemporary cloud-based or on-premises systems previously discussed.

CHAPTER 7
Low cost Accounting Software

We have discussed Integrated Accounting Systems for Medium and Small Business. Apart from them, there are many simple to use, low cost Accounting Software for small business, providing core and essential accounting functions like, Financial Accounting Books & Statements, Invoicing & Inventory, targeted for small organisations. Some of them even provide FREE basic module to start with, and option to upgrade to higher module, on payment of low charges.

Cost of these software solutions is significantly lower than those previously mentioned. They are affordable for small organizations, offer user-friendly experience and straightforward implementation advantage. These software applications incorporate advanced features of Workflow Automation, enabling instant communication of business information directly within the system during operations. They deliver robust invoicing capabilities, fundamental accounting functions, and inventory reporting, enhancing operational efficiency.

Organizations that are new to implementing a computerised business accounting system, should consider these solutions for their initial deployment, before transitioning to larger, costlier and more complex systems, outlined in earlier section.

General Features and Customization

To Enhance user flexibility and ensure compatibility with existing data management systems.

- **Custom Fields and Branding:** Document customisation, Customized Company logos, Invoice Themes, user-defined fields to create a professional and personalized business image.
- **Data Import and Integration:** Data Mapping and Import from Excel sheet.
- **Workflow Automation:** Document progression, hierarchical approvals through user defined workflow cycle.
- **Documents and Reports Sharing:** Documents and Reports instant sharing and via WhatsApp, SMS, social media channels.

Reporting and Data Sharing

Actionable Reports, through notifications, messages and information sharing

- **Configurable Reports:** Filtered, summarized, and detailed reports for sales, purchases, and stock.
- **Digital Sharing and Printing:** Saving reports in digital formats and printing for easy access and communication.
- **Graphical Insights:** Visual graphs, Infographics

Invoicing and Billing

Simplified Invoicing & Tax Billing

- **Customizable Invoicing:** Multiple Invoice layouts, auto-numbering, user-defined fields, terms and conditions, digital sharing via SMS, WhatsApp, or email.
- **GST Invoicing:** Automated GST Computation in Invoice, e-way bills, e-invoices with QR codes, IRN embedding,
- **GST Accounting:** GST reconciliation, mismatch correction, GSTR-1, GSTR-2, GSTR-3B and GST Annual Returns Filing

PoS and Payment Management

Quick multiple invoicing & payment options.

- **Real-Time PoS Features:** Multiple simultaneous PoS invoicing, barcode scanning, receipt printers, cash drawers.

- **Flexible Payment Modes:** Multiple payments modes, Loyalty & reward points offers and redemption.

Inventory Management

Inventory flow and stock tracking for stock-outs, overstocking, obsolesce, expired goods,

- **Inventory Control:** Real-time stock tracking with alerts for low stock, batch and expiry management, and inter-store transfers.
- **Auto Replenishment:** Automated replenishment orders generation, based on inventory levels and purchase orders.
- **Stock Item Tracking:** Barcode scanning, serial number generation for Item level tracking and control.

Financial Accounting and Reporting

Financial Accounting & Financial Management

- **Core Accounting Features:** Chart of accounts, multi-debit/credit vouchers, expense tracking, bank reconciliation, audit trails.
- **Receivables and Payables Management:** Outstanding bills with aging reports, reminders, area-wise / city-wise analysis.
- **Financial Management:** Financial Statements, Cash & Fund Flow, Performance Ratio,

Sales, Purchase, and Profit Analysis

Sales Accounting & Sales Promotion

- **Sales & Purchase Tracking:** Periodical summaries and detailed transaction reports, item-wise profitability, & party-wise sales, purchase analytics.
- **Sales Promotion:** Targeted marketing campaigns, promotions, discounts, new product launches.
- **Trend Analysis:** Sales & Purchase history and trends, identify opportunities performance improvements.

These systems prioritize quick and efficient invoicing while providing essential integration with accounting and inventory modules, ensuring small businesses maintain operational efficiency, compliance, and data accuracy.

Popular Low Cost Accounting Software

- Khata Billing
- Kuber Accounting
- My Bill Book

Khata Billng

Khata Billing is a cloud based Accounting, GST Invoicing & Inventory Software. It may be registered free through email id and start working. Khata Billing Invoicing & Inventory Basic Plan is Free.

Functionalities

- **Quotation & Estimates:** Quotations with GST and other terms, Quotations Convert to Invoice, on line sharing through SMS, WhatsApp, email.
- **Invoicing:** Customisable Invoice theme, Multiple Invoice Layout with customisable Logo, Invoice Signature, Sales Reports, Invoice Printing / Sharing, Price List, Sale Summary, Item wise sales, Partywise Sales,
- **PoS:** Printed or digital Invoice, configurable discounts, connected receipt printer, barcode scanner, cash drawer.
- **Sales Analysis:** Sales Revenue, Cost & Profit Summaries & Detailed Reports, Sales Trends, Item Profitability, Sales History Trails, Sales Reports export to Excel,
- **Expenses:** Expense recording, Expense details, Accountwise Expense statement.
- **GST:** GST Invoicing, GST Calculator, GST Reports and GST Returns.
- **Inventory:** Real Time Inventory Tracking, Inventory Alerts, Auto Ordering for Stock replenishments, Materials Receipts against Purchase Orders, Inter Stores Transfers, Stock reports, Bar Coded Item Labels Printing, Stock Transfers and Stock Adjustment,
- **Reports:** Accounts Receivables, PL Statement,
- **Workflow:** Stagewise documents approval and conversion from Quotation, Order, Sales to Accounts

Module Pricing

- **Free Module:** Invoicing & Inventory only, Khata Billing Branding on Invoice and Messages, No GST reports, No thermal printer, Ads during operation,
- **Premium Module (Rs 999 / year):** All Modules, Ads Free, No Branding in Invoice or Message, Money back Guarantee within 15 days.

Kuber Accounting

Kuber Accounting is premises based software for Accounting, GST Billing & Inventory management,

Features

- **Financial Accounting:** Chart of Accounts, Multi Debit / Credit Voucher Entry, Cheque Details in Voucher, Voucher Narration Entry & Carry from another Voucher, Voucher Audit, Documents Attachment, Voucher sharing through SMS, Voucher Print/ Share in Excel,
- **Accounting Reports:** Journal Voucher, Day Books, Cash Bank Books, Journal Book, Ledger Books, Accounts Confirmation Reports, Bank Reconciliation, Monthly Figures Graphs,
- **Receivables & Payables:** Open Bills Reports, Ageing Reports, City / Areawise Reports, Reminder Letters,
- **Reporting Features:** Filter through Date Range, Periodical Summaries,
- **Sales Invoice:** Cash Sales, Credit Sales, User Defined Fields, Series / Auto Numbering, User defined Product Description in Invoice, Returned Item in Invoice, Alternate UoM in Invoice, Batch / Expiry Date, Multiple Godown, Price List, Additional Charges in Invoice, Invoice Narration, Terms & Conditions,
- **Purchase Bills:** Cash Purchase, Credit Sales, User Defined Fields, Returned Item in Invoice, Alternate UoM in Invoice, Batch / Expiry Date, Multiple Godown, Additional Charges in Invoice, Invoice Narration,
- **Sales Purchase Reports:** Sales & Purchase Periodical Summaries, Partywise sales / Purchase Analysis, Productwise / party wise / Party Wise Productwise Analysis,

- **Stock Management:** Stock Ledgers, Stock Reports, Stock Summaries, Batch / Expiry Date Reports,
- **GST:** GSR Rceoncilation, GST Mismatch, GSTR-1, GSTR-2, GSTR-3B, GSTR-4,

All modules of Kuber Software may be downloaded from vendors website for review.

My Bill Book

My Bill Book is Cloud Accounting System covering Financial Accounting, GST Invoicing & Inventory Software. It is accessible on SmartPhone also.

Features

- **General:** Company Logo, Custom Fields, Data import from Excel,
- **Sales Promotion:** Targeted marketing through fast Communication of Price, Discounts, Sales Schemes, Festival & Promotional Sales, New Products, SMS Campaign,
- **Inventory:** Pre loaded Multi Level Stock Group / Category Items masters, Batch Number & Expiry, Bar Code Scan and label Print, Item unique Serial Number, Stock Level Alerts, Custom Attributes in Stock Items, Multiple Godowns,
- **Invoicing:** Customised Invoice Format, e-way Bill, e-Invoice, QR Code and IRN embedding,
- **PoS:** Multiple simultaneous POS Invoicing, SMS Invoice, WhatsApp / Facebook customer order integration & Messaging, Bar Code scanning, Multiple Payment Mode, Plain & Roll Printers,
- **Accounts:** Chart of Accounts, Vouchers, Accounts Books, Accounts Receivables & Payables & Ageing, Bank Reconciliation,
- **GST Accounting:** Company GST profile, GST Invoicing, e-Way Bills, e-Invoicing, GSTR Reports Filing,
- **Employee Payroll:** Employee Master, Pay Structure, Attendance, Payroll Computation, Paylip, Pay Register and other Pay Reports.

Pricing:

- **Desktop:** Monthly Rates, Billed Annually. Multiple Devices.
    - o **FREE:** Basic Invoicing only.

- **Diamond:** Rs 217 / month, only on line, 1 Business, 3 User + 1 CA, Customised Invoice, Accounting,
- **Platinum:** Rs 250 / moth, On-line + Off Line (Desktop), 2 Business, 3 User + 1CA, upto 50 e-way Bills / year, upto 500 SMS, Payroll, Multiple Godown, Bar Code Printing, WhatsApp & SMS marketing,
- **Enterprise:** Rs 417 / month, On-line + Off Line (Desktop), 2 Business, Unlimited Users + 1CA, e-Invoicing, unlimited e-way Bills, Recurring Bills, POS, Loyalty & Rewards, Inventory with Multiple Godowns, Payroll, Bar Code Printing, WhatsApp & SMS marketing, Data Export to Tally,

- **Mobile:** Billing Software on Mobile App on Android, iOS, Web at Rs 399 annual, 1 Business, 1 device, 1 user.

CHAPTER 8
GST Invoicing & Accounting software

In our previous discussions, we explored various aspects of Accounting Systems tailored for Small and Medium Enterprises. Now, we turn attention to software solutions specifically designed for small traders, with a focus on GST-compliant invoicing, GST reporting and filing, accessible via both smartphones and computers.

User-Friendly Free Applications

These accounting applications are predominantly available at no cost for basic features, with minimal licensing fees for advanced functionalities. Built on cutting-edge platforms, most of these applications are compatible with smartphones and tablets, facilitating remote access to accounting tasks. They provide an innovative accounting experience, enabling non-accountants and individuals with basic smartphone skills to work effortlessly.

Practical Tools for Learning Computerized Accounting

For organizations considering the implementation of a computerized accounting system or individuals seeking practical experience, utilizing such an application (preferably a free one) is an excellent starting point. This hands-on experience will provide valuable insights into the implementation of an Accounting System, making the transition to more feature-rich desktop applications seamless and efficient.

Free GST Software for GST registered organisation

GSTN Organization has empaneled few GST Billing & Accounting software, both on-line & offline. GST registered organisation having turnover upto 1.5 crores may download free from the GST Portal on login with necessary particulars, and use them. The basic modules are free, but you may have to pay for advanced features. The use policy may vary from organisation to organisation. Check the respective sites of the developer.

Downloading Free GST Software from GSTN website

Login to GSTN Portal entering the credentials. Navigate to Downloads > Accounting and Billing Software option. Type Yes at "Is your turnover < 1.5 Crores". Select the Software to be downloaded from the list. Read and accept Disclaimer. At GSTN Form, enter the Particulars. OTP will be sent to registered email id. Enter OTP and proceed to download the software. A registration confirmation will be received in the email. Now start working.

Apart from Apps available in GSTN Portal, many other Apps are also available, as discussed next

GST Invoicing & Accounting Software Key Features

General Controls

- Multi Company, Multi User, Multi Currency
- Bulk Upload of Data, Reports / Data Export in Excel, Master Data Import / Export from and To External App. Export Reports to Excel, PDF, CSV, XML, Data Migration to Tally, Data Mapping with external App for Data Import / Export, Customisable Templates for Masters Data Import

- Thermal printer / Bar Code scanner Integration
- Role based user rights, Logo and e-sign in Documents and Reports, User Activity log, Audit Trail
- Document Sequencing, Multiple Voucher Series & Numbering, Document attachments to Vouchers, User defined Fields in Forms and Reports
- Reports Drill-down
- Documents sharing on WhatsApp, e-mail
- Integration with Tally
- Online payment gateways
- Workflow and Document Conversion, Document Duplication
- Activity Log, Audit Trail

Accounts

- Masters Data Creation, Opening Balance Entry / Carrying from Previous year Accounts, Import Masters Data from Previous year Accounts,
- Accounts Vouchers, Payments & Receipts, Cheque Printing
- Cash and Bank Books, Accounting Books, Statements & Reports, Income / Expense report
- Accounts Receivables & Payables, Receivables and Payables tracking, Payment Reminders, Outstanding Bills Age Analysis, MSME Report
- Trial Balance, Profit and Loss account, Balance Sheet
- Track Payments/ expenses,

Invoicing

- Multiple Document Format Template,
- Purchase Order, Sales Order, Quotation, Estimates, Order tracking
- Proforma Invoice, Delivery Challan, Credit / Debit Notes, Recurring Invoice / subscription
- Purchase / Sales invoice, Small (A5) Invoice template, Shipping Label
- Automated Invoice Computation, Invoice Terms & Conditions
- Multiple Price Lists

- Print / Email / SMS Share Invoice
- PoS

GST

- GST UOMs, E-invoice, e-way Bills, Manual & Bulk e-Way Bill generation in JSON, GST Calculator, Multiple GSTN, Stock Item HSN mapping
- GST Returns in Excel & JSON,
- Excel/ JSON File for GST Portal upload
- Upload to GST Portal through offline tool
- GST Invoice data export to XLS / JSON format
- Export / SEZ Invoice
- E-Way Bill, E-Invoice

Inventory

- Stock Item Masters, Import Inventory Master from Other applications
- Multi Level Stock Group & Category;
- Simple, Dual & Compound Unit of Measurement
- Barcode Generation / Labels Printing,
- Inventory status / Inventory Tracking, Stock Level alerts
- Materials Transactions and Stock Reports
- Inventory Reports & Analytics,
- Item wise, customer wise sales reports & analysis and summary
- Item wise Gross Profit
- Stock Item Batch / Godown / Expiry, Product Attributes

Popular GST Invoicing & Accounting Software at GST Portal

We now briefly discuss the key features of following GST Invoicing Software, down loadable from GST Portal.

uBooks, FACE, FocusLyte, CaptainBiz,

uBooks

uBooks is Cloud based GST Compliant Invoicing Software, accessible in Mobile (Android & iOS) & Desktop (Web)

Key Features

Multiple Companies & Users, GST UOMs, Bulk Upload of Stock Items Data, E-invoice, e-way Bills, GST Calculator, Bar Code, Multiple Invoice templates, Invoice sharing over WhatsApp/ Email, Inventory Levels, GST Return Ready Reports for filing, Reports / Data Export in Excel, Data Import in Tally,

WhatsApp integration, supports Thermal printer,

Pricing: Rs 1555 for 3 months, 4999 for 1 year, Dedicated Phone support

14 days FREE Trial.

FACE

Cygnet FACE is On-Premises Invoicing, Accounting & GST compliant Software, running on Windows, under Microsoft .NET framework.

Key Features

Multi Company, Multi User, Multiple GSTN (under single PAN), Multi Currency, e-way Bill, Bar Code scanner, Stock Item HSN mapping, Excel File for Master Import, e-Invoice, Excel / JSON File for GST Portal upload. MSME Report, Role based user rights, Document attachments, Logo and e-sign, User Activity log, Audit Trail, Multiple Voucher Series & Numbering, Accounting Books, Accounting Statements & Reports,

Pricing: One Time Rs.17750 (or Rs.9750 Annual).

FocusLyte

FocusLyte is cloud based on line Invoicing and GST Compliant Accounting Software.

Key Features

- Sales and Purchase orders, Orders tracking
- Invoice Specific Terms & Conditions, Automated Invoice Computation, Multiple Price Lists, Invoice SMS, Print / Email / Share Invoice

- Multi-Entity (Multi GSTIN) for single company, Manual and Bulk E-way Bill generation, GSTR-2 Reconciliation, GSTR-2A Reconciliation, GSTR-3B, GST Returns filing
- e-Way Bill Print, JSON & SMS options, Bulk e-Way Bill generation in JSON, Import/Export XML Data for GST, GST Returns in Excel & JSON for upload.
- Receivables and Payables tracking, Outstanding Bills Age Analysis,
- Barcode Generation / Labels Printing, Inventory status / Inventory management
- Document Sequencing, Compound Unit of Measurement, Barcode Scanning, User defined Fields in Forms and Reports, Reports Drill-down, Trial Balance, Profit and Loss account, Balance Sheet, Export Reports to Excel, PDF, CSV, XML, Cost Center / Salesman / Warehouse masters & transaction analysis, Post Dated Cheques, Bank Reconciliation, Report layout customisation, CA login Edit & View options for multiple companies

Pricing: Rs 3000 per annum.

CaptainBiz

CaptainViz is Cloud based GST Compliant Invoicing Software.

Key Features

- Multi Company Multi User,
- Import GSTIN based Customer Data from previous filed GST reports, Import/ Export Data of Masters from Previous year Accounts, with Opening Balance, Customisable Templates for Masters Data Import.
- Purchase / Sales Orders, Order tracking, Delivery Challans,
- Customized Invoice template, E-Way Bill, E-Invoice generation & sharing with customers, Purchase / Sales invoice, Materials Transactions and Stock Reports,
- Payments & Receipts, Cash and Bank account tracking, Accounts Receivables & Payables,
- Inventory Tracking, Bar Code Scanner, Data Migration to Tally with data Integrity Check, Data Mapping with Tally, Data Export, record of exported Data, Data error Handling for report generation in Tally. It acts as support system to Tally.
- GSTR Reports including GSTR1, GSTR 3B, and GSTR4

14 Days Free Trial, Mobile App Android / iOS, Desktop on Windows.

Pricing: 1555 for 3 months, 4999 for 1 year.

We have already covered GST Invoicing module for Saral Accounting, ZOHO Invoice, Vyapar and Marg covered in earlier chapters. See the current policy of use, in the respective website.

Other popular GST Invoicing & Accounting Software

Apart from the above software available in GST Portal, the following are popular low cost Invoicing and Accounting Software. Brief details of these software are given here.

- Clear One
- SleekBill
- Swipe
- GoGSTBill

ClearOne

ClearOne is Cloud based Free GST invoicing software; workable on a desktop PC, laptop, mobile, and iPad; It tracks receivables and payables, set payment reminders, and send payment reminders via WhatsApp, SMS, and email. Some modules are available free for a limited Trial period.

Key Features

- Customise GST Bills with pre created templates
- Create & share Quotations, Orders, E-way Bills, Delivery challans, Tax Invoice, Bill of Supply, etc, and share digitally with customers.
- Online payment & collection through Netbanking, UPI, payments links via SMS, WhatsApp, email etc. Payment Reminders,
- On-line, real time inventory management, Inventory Reports & Analytics,
- Stock Level alerts,

Sleek Bill

Sleek Bill is Cloud based On-line & Premises based Offline Invoicing & Inventory software.

Key Features:

- **Invoicing:** Proforma Invoice, Delivery Challan, Credit / Debit Notes, Small (A5) Invoice template, Itemwise, customerwise sales reports & analysis and summary, Itemwise Gross Profit,
- **Inventory:** Multi Level Stock Group & Category, Alternate & Compound UoM, Inventory In / Out & Stock in Hand, Inventory levels alerts,
- **Workflow:** Convert Orders to Delivery / Receipt Notes to Invoice without data entry,
- **GST Compliance:** Tax Invoice, E-way bills with GSTIN, HSN / SAC details, GSTR 1, 3B & 4 Reports in compliant excel format, Upload to GST Portal through offline tool, Invoice data export to XLS / JSON format.

Pricing

- **Offline FREE:** 10 documents /month, One design template, Basic Invoicing features, Basic GST features, No dedicated support.
- **Offline Invoicing:** 2360 / annum: GST template & Invoice customisation, Small A5 Invoice format, Quotation, Proforma Invoice, Delivery Notes, Tax Invoice, Bill of Supply, Unlimited documents, Product level discount, Payment link in Invoice, SEZ options, GST Inclusive / exclusive Billing, Multi Currency Export Invoice, e-mail support,
- **Offline Invoicing + Inventory:** 3775 / annum. All Offline Invoicing features + Multi copy Invoice (Original, Duplicate...etc), Transport Document / e-Way Bill, Master Data Import / Export, XLS / JSON file export for GST upload,
- **Online Invoicing + Inventory:** 3539 / annum. On-line access to any device, Secured Auto Data Back Up, e-Invoice, data migration from Offline to On-line system,

15 days FREE Trial

Swipe

Swipe is GST compliant on-premises Invoicing & Inventory software for billing, payments, and online stores. It is available in Windows & MacOS on Desktop, and in Android & IOS on Mobile.

Key Features

Multiple Users, Role Based user rights, Integration with Tally, Thermal Printer connectivity,

Quotation / Estimates, Invoice, purchase orders in Multiple formats, share documents on WhatsApp/ Email, Customized Invoices, online payment gateways, Manage Inventory, Track Payments/ expenses, PoS, Stock Item Batch / Expiry in Invoice, Product Attributes, Accounts Receivables, Payment Reminders,

E-Way bills. Tax Invoice, Bill of Supply, E-Invoice, Export / SEZ Invoice, recurring Invoice / subscription, GST Reports, Online store with product details, images/ banners /offers/ categories/ banners, SMS campaign, etc

Pricing

- **FREE:** 1 User, 1 Business, Quotation, Invoicing, Inventory, 1 Invoice Format, SWIPE Branding in Documents,
- **PRO:** Rs 2799 / annum, 1 User, 1 Business, Everything in FREE Plan+ No Swipe logo on Bills. Multiple Invoice templates, Online Payment Gateways, GSTR Reports, Product Variants, Custom fields/ columns & charges, Bulk uploads of customers, vendors & products, Custom header/ footer/ watermark, Workflow to Convert documents, Priority Support, iOS App access
- **JET:** Rs 3699/ annum, 2 Users, 1 Business, Everything in PRO Plan + E-way bills, Bulk downloads, 1GB Swipe Drive, Multiple Price List, User Activity Log, Bulk Edit.
- **RISE:** Rs 4999/ annum, Everything in JET Plan + POS Billing, Batch & Expiry, Subscription/ Recurring Billing, Bank Reconciliation.

Advanced BIZ plan for additional customised features.

GoGSTBill

GoGSTBill is Cloud based on-line GST billing software, works on Desktop & Mobile.

Features

- Customer & Product, Import Customer / Product,
- Quotation, Proforma Invoice, Delivery Challan, Purchase Order, Sale Order, Sales & Purchase Invoice, Payment Receipt,
- GST Reports, Inventory Reports, Cheque Printing,

- Documents Share on WhatsApp / e-mail, E-Way Bill, E-Invoice, Credit / Debit Note,
- Export / SEZ Invoices, Daily Income / Expense report,
- Invoice Header Design, Multiple Invoice Template, Shipping Label, Workflow Document Conversion, Document Duplication, Thermal Printer Integration, Barcode Scanning,
- Custom Column & Field in Documents, Activity Log, Documents sharing on WhatsApp.

Pricing

- **FREE:** Max 25 Items in Invoice, Max 3000 docs / annum,
- **PREMIUM:** 1499 / annum, Max 250 Items In Doc, Max 15000 Doc. / Year

CHAPTER 9
AI Accounting Software & Tools

Harnessing Artificial Intelligence for Business Accounting Efficiency

AI accounting software is transforming financial management by providing automation, predictive insights, and enhanced security. Despite the challenges associated with its adoption, the advantages significantly surpass the initial investment and learning curve. By optimizing operations, enhancing compliance, and delivering actionable insights, AI equips businesses to make informed decisions, mitigate risks, and enhance profitability. As AI technology continues to advance, its significance in accounting will expand, establishing it as an essential tool for enterprises poised for the future. Some examples of application of AI in Accounting may be cited as:

- **Task Automation:** AI streamlines routine tasks such as data entry, reconciliation, and report generation, thereby reducing manual labour and enhancing accuracy. Such automation allows employees to dedicate their time to more complex analytical tasks, ultimately boosting overall productivity. AI's sophisticated algorithms can identify irregularities more swiftly than manual processes, thereby diminishing fraud risks and enhancing transparency within organizations.

- **Large Data Analysis:** AI supports accountants in swiftly and accurately analyzing extensive volumes of financial data. Machine learning algorithms empower businesses to process vast amounts of information in real-time and forecast trends, facilitating timely adjustments and informed decision-making based on precise predictions. Advanced analytics tools also enable companies to pinpoint areas needing improvement, allowing them to address potential issues before they escalate.
- **Multi-Platform Integration:** AI facilitates seamless integration with existing accounting systems, thereby eliminating duplicate entries and minimizing human error. This reduction in redundancy conserves both time and resources, while fostering consistency across all departments. Furthermore, AI Automated reporting ensures compliance with regulatory requirements.
- **Future Planning & Forecasting:** AI significantly enhances financial planning and forecasting capabilities. Organizations can utilize machine learning models to anticipate economic fluctuations, assess investment opportunities, optimize inventory management, and establish optimal pricing strategies. With improved forecasting capabilities, businesses can make proactive strategic decisions rather than merely responding to changing market conditions.

Incorporating AI into business accounting practices yields numerous benefits, including increased productivity, reduced costs, and enhanced data analysis and decision-making. As AI technology continues to evolve, further advancements in these areas are anticipated, leading to improved accounting efficiency and effectiveness. Consequently, the adoption of AI solutions is imperative for businesses aiming to remain competitive and sustain financial stability in today's rapidly evolving economy.

Key Features of AI Accounting Software

AI-based accounting software combines machine learning, natural language processing (NLP), and real-time data analytics to provide a comprehensive business management solution.

Core Functionalities

- **Predictive Analytics and Forecasting:** Uses advanced algorithms to predict future financial trends and cash flow scenarios.

- **Automated Bookkeeping:** Categorizes financial data and performs routine bookkeeping tasks like invoicing, payroll, and reconciliation.
- **Fraud Detection:** Detects anomalies in transactions and raises real-time alerts for potential fraud or irregularities.
- **Tax Compliance:** Automates tax filings, calculations, and compliance checks to minimize human error.
- **Customizable Dashboards:** Real-time visualization of financial data for monitoring performance and trends.

Additional Features

- **Virtual Assistance:** AI-powered chatbots to handle queries and perform tasks like expense reporting and invoice processing.
- **Integration Capabilities:** Seamlessly connects with other accounting tools and ERP systems.
- **Security Enhancements:** AI identifies suspicious activities, ensuring data integrity and compliance with privacy regulations.

Thus, AI-based accounting software excels in automating mundane tasks, providing predictive insights, and enhancing security. Its capabilities extend beyond traditional accounting by enabling businesses to make proactive, data-driven decisions.

Benefits of AI Accounting Software

AI accounting software drives efficiency, accuracy, and cost-effectiveness while reducing manual effort.

Operational Advantages

- **Automation:** Eliminates repetitive tasks like data entry, freeing up resources for strategic activities.
- **Error Reduction:** AI algorithms minimize human errors in financial processes.
- **Real-Time Insights:** Offers instantaneous analysis and reporting for informed decision-making.

Cost and Time Savings

- **Reduced Labor Costs:** Automates processes, lowering dependency on manual labor.

- **Time Efficiency:** Accelerates tasks like reconciliation and report generation.
- **Enhanced Resource Utilization:** Redirects human resources to more value-added tasks.

Strategic Benefits

- **Fraud Prevention:** Real-time detection and prevention of financial irregularities.
- **Actionable Insights:** Identifies patterns in financial data, enabling better budgeting and expense management.
- **Improved Compliance:** Ensures adherence to tax and regulatory requirements.

Use Cases of AI Accounting Software

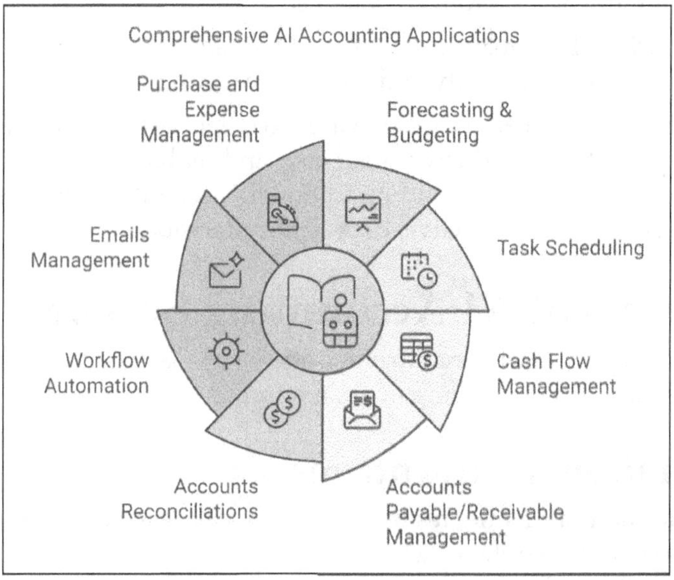

AI has versatile applications in accounting and finance, catering to a broad range of business needs.

Forecasting & Budgeting

- Predictive analytics to anticipate revenue trends, budget requirements, and potential financial risks.
- Analyzing historical data to identify seasonal patterns and market dynamics.

- Simulating financial scenarios for strategic planning and investments.
- Create accurate budgets by analyzing historical data, considering various scenarios.

Scheduling

- Automating calendar management, including meetings, client deadlines and compliance reminders.
- Allocating resources efficiently based on workload projections and deadlines.
- Workforce scheduling for optimal productivity.

Managing Cash Flow

- Monitoring real-time cash flow metrics to provide actionable insights and alerts.
- Predicting cash shortfalls or surpluses by analyzing cash inflow and outflow trends.
- Optimizing payment cycles and debt management.

Accounts payable/receivable:

- Automated data extraction from invoices,
- Verify accuracy and routing for approval or payment
- Streamline accounts payable and receivable.

Accounts reconciliations:

- Transactions matching, discrepancies identification
- Automate reconciliations generation

Workflow Automation

- Automate routine tasks like data entry, reconciliations, and reporting.
- Create client specific workflows.
- Enhanced operational efficiency through rule-based workflows.

Emails Management

- Drafting professional responses to routine client queries using natural language processing.
- Prioritizing important emails and filtering spam for improved productivity.
- Analyzing email patterns to predict client needs or highlight urgent matters.

Purchase and Expense Management

- Automating purchase approvals by extracting data from scanned or digital invoices.
- Categorizing and reconciling expenses for analysis and audit.
- Proper record-keeping for Tax regulations and compliance

Data Analysis

- Analyzing large datasets for trends in financial performance.
- Benchmarking against industry standards to identify areas for improvement.
- Visualizing data in interactive dashboards for enhanced decision-making.

Business Communication

- Automated Reports and summaries generation.
- Improved communication through AI-powered tools (like chatbots and real-time translations).

Project Management

- Assigning tasks and tracking progress with AI-driven project management tools.
- Identifying bottlenecks and recommending solutions for improved efficiency.
- Dynamic and real time Project timelines changes.

Fraud Detection

- Identifying suspicious patterns using NLP and anomaly detection.

Client service:

- AI-driven chatbots or virtual assistants to provide 24/7 support to clients,
- Answering common questions and account inquiries.

The diverse use cases of AI in accounting, make it a powerful tool for businesses. From daily operations to strategic planning, AI accounting software supports efficiency and accuracy across multiple financial processes. Its ability to provide actionable insights ensures businesses remain agile and competitive.

Challenges in Implementing AI Accounting Software

While AI accounting software offers significant advantages, there are challenges to its implementation and usage.

Technical Challenges

- **Integration Complexity:** Merging AI tools with existing accounting systems can be time-consuming.
- **Data Quality:** AI's accuracy depends on the quality and completeness of input data.

Cost and Expertise

- **High Initial Investment:** AI tools can require substantial upfront costs for licensing and setup.
- **Skill Gap:** Specialized knowledge is needed to operate and maintain AI-based systems.

Cultural and Ethical Concerns

- **Resistance to Change:** Employees may fear job loss or loss of control over financial processes.
- **Bias in Algorithms:** Ensuring AI systems are trained on unbiased, representative data is critical.
- **Privacy and Security Risks:** Businesses must comply with data protection laws and ensure sensitive information is safeguarded.

Despite its challenges, AI accounting software offers unparalleled advantages. Mitigating risks through proper training, robust security measures, and gradual adoption can lead to successful implementation.

Factors for Selection of right AI Accounting Software

Many accounting software companies claim to use artificial intelligence (AI) in some way to enhance their products. However, AI implementation vary widely between different accounting software. Also, the level of AI automation and decision-making can be different. So it's important to research each product and determine what features are best suited to your business needs. Choosing the right AI-based accounting software involves considering several critical factors:

Business Needs and Features

- Ensure the software aligns with your company's specific requirements, such as invoicing or payroll management.
- Look for scalability to adapt to your business's growth and evolving needs.

Usability and Support

- Prioritize user-friendly interfaces for seamless adoption.
- Evaluate the quality of customer support and availability of resources for training.

Integration and Compliance

- Verify compatibility with existing systems.
- Ensure adherence to regulatory standards for financial reporting and data protection.

Cost and Vendor Reputation

- Balance cost-effectiveness with quality and features.
- Choose vendors with positive reviews and proven track records in AI-based accounting solutions.

Selecting the right AI Accounting Tools involves understanding your business needs, evaluating usability, and considering integration and cost. A thoughtful selection process ensures maximum ROI and long-term benefits.

AI Accounting Software Overview

Now we discuss salient features of some popular AI accounting software. This will help you to understand what AI software offers, distinct from traditional non-ai accounting software. It will also help you to evaluate AI software, and select a right one, for your specific needs.

Gridlex Sky

Gridlex Sky AI accounting software, to make financial processes more efficient.

- intuitive interface and advanced analytics capabilities.
- automate processes such as invoicing, credit control, reconciliation, budgeting, and forecasting,
- In-built AI-driven financial advisers like, AI profit advisor, AI revenue advisor, AI expense advisor, and AI inventory advisor to aid controlling and streamlining day-to-day business activities.
- Automated routine bulk tasks like data entry, invoice reconciliation, and reporting.
- Predictive models to identify potential future issues
- Detailed analysis of customer trends and spending patterns, for optimum resources allocation.

VIC.ai

- Automates extraction of data from invoices, coding, approvals, workflows, PO matching.
- Intelligent dashboard featuring real-time data analytics utilizing data mining processes to improve ROI and offer full control of finances.
- Insights into spending patterns for strategic financial planning.
- Automated Accounts Payable and Accounts Receivable processes
- Cross-check expenses against company policies and compliance rules, flagging discrepancies and violations.
- Audit trails for financial audits and compliance checks.

- Self learning & training from work performance to automate correct processes, approvals and decisions. So, over time, with continued learning from outline transactions, AI performs better than before.
- Open API to integrate and work with popular accounting platforms, like QuickBooks, Sage Intacct, and other ERP systems

ZENI.ai

- Designed for small and medium-sized businesses manage financial operations.
- Automates bulk routine tasks of bookkeeping and other accounting tasks
- Automated classification of transactions, data extraction to streamline accounting process.
- AI-powered dashboard to get deeper insights of the business
- Overview of key financial metrics such as cash flow, expenses, and revenues.
- Visual data presentation through charts and graphs
- Customizable dashboards to real time display data relevant to user, drill down to relevant details
- Spot expense trends across the entire business and flag anything that is going wrong.

Bill.ai

- Accounts receivable and payable automation platform to streamline AR/AP processes.
- automates the bill-creation process by extracting invoice and vendor information from documents
- Offers credit and expense management software known as Divvy From Bill, as follows:
    - Divvy from Bill is AI-powered expense management and budgeting software for businesses to automate their financial processes, including expenses, invoicing, and payments.
    - It uses machine learning and natural language processing to automate tasks of receipt categorization and vendor payment matching, generates expense reports.

- o Its expense management software provides fast reconciliation and reporting of expenses.
- o Using Divvy chip card, employees can make purchases, and the expenses are notified to company in real-time.
- o Divvy budgeting software controls expenses by setting spending limits
- o syncs with cards and providing real-time visibility of spending, analysed by department, team, project, or individual budget.
- o create multiple budgets for different departments, teams, or projects; request and send funds instantly from mobile or desktop devices.

Docyt

- Reads, understands and extracts relevant information from various transaction documents. Substantially reduces bulky & mundane manual tasks
- Generates personalized and informative financial reports.
- Works in conjunction with QuickBooks
- Contextualizes and summarizes internal and external information into actions.
- categorizes major transactions use of generative AI
- Automated reconciliation of transactions with Bank and between various accounting books and reports.
- Through self learning and technology of AI, it learns the user's business over times, to automate the back office tasks.

Botkeeper

- Automated bookkeeping support using combination of machine learning, artificial intelligence, and skilled accountants.
- automate bookkeeping function, collecting data from various sources, to provide insightful reporting and dashboard features.
- Expert accounting team to monitor automation and focus on complex accounting, data integrity, and interpretation.

Rows AI

AI empowered spreadsheet editor to analyze, summarize and transform data, directly with OpenAI

- Simplifies and cleans up data, summarize the key takeaways from dataset.
- Extract data trends and patterns.
- Tag and classify any type of text automatically.